Chapel Services For Sports Teams

This book is non-fiction and is based on the Bible (NIV & KJV).

Publishing date 10/16/2018

Produced by 2911 Publishing Company ISBN

#9781728876337

Copyright filed 10/10/2018 in U.S. Copyright Offices

FORWARD

This book was written for anyone conducting a team chapel service, regardless of the sport. Designed for quick outline or an easy access guide to specific topics, this format will accommodate both the seasoned and novice alike.

1. Select the topic from the TABLE OF CONTENTS.
2. Review the story or outline.
3. Begin and end your chapels with prayer and scripture. This will encourage your athletes to join the discussion more freely.

Focusing on God's Grace and Mercy through Christ will always prove to carry a positive note from beginning to end.

All the chapels within this book are intended to help motivate, encourage, and to be a guiding light for your athletes.

Yours in Christ,
Jim Gillespie,
Chaplain

A Special Dedication…

Mr. Reggie Speak has always been a very special brother in Christ, ever since we met in the Quad Cities of Iowa for CBA. He remains an inspiration and encouragement to my continuance of sports chapels and as a former walking / prayer partner as well as my great Sunday school teacher, he remains my example and I am proud to call him my friend.

Respected as a distinguished athletic trainer, teacher, and physical therapist, Reggie, now re- tired at the early age of 87 years (young). He still heartens me to have served as Chaplain for many teams. His faith and dedication to family have carried me through the years allowing me to follow in his footsteps. I am grateful for the honor of knowing him. God bless you, Reggie, and thank you for being my mentor…. Additional appreciation to Rod and Susan Brown.

Chapel Services For Sports Teams

By: Jim Gillespie

TABLE OF CONTENTS

CHAPELS   **Page**

1. Bible Explanation   12

2. Holy Bible Facts   15

3. Name Above All Names   19

4. Remember Today   24

5. God's Answers to Satan's Lies   25

6. Pray   29

7. Keep it R.E.A.L.   31

8. Power of Prayer   33

9. James 4:2   34

10. Pray For Your Pastor   37

11. Three Levels of Prayer   39

12. A.S.K. Matthew 7:7   41

13. 5 Suggestions For A Great Prayer   45

14. The Lord's Prayer   47

15. James Jones: A Great Success Story   50

16. The Greatest Super Bowl Ever Played   54

17. Veterans Day   56

18. Bible Emergency Phone Numbers   58

19. God Honors His Servants   62

20. 23rd Psalm   64

21. God Hears Your Prayer   68

22. One Solitary Life   70

23. The Athlete's Prayer   73

24. David – A Man After God's Own Heart   75

25. God's Spoken Ministry   76

26. The Value of Hard Places   77

27. Trade "I Can't" For "I CAN, I Will, I DID!"   80

28. 1 Thessalonians 1: 2-3   81

29. The Way To Live Your Life   82

30. Things You Can Control   83

31. What You Believe Is Critical   84

32. 7 Ways To Become A Godly Man   86

33. You Were Created To Serve Others   88

34. Don't Quit Poem   90

35. 10 Things God Wants You To Remember   92

36. The Christian Warrior   94

37. Never Say Never   97

38. Mother's Day   98

39. Praising God All the Time   99

40. Sanctification   100

41. John's Gospel (Who Jesus Is)   104

42. John's Gospel (It Is Finished)   106

43. Less Is Not More   109

44. Be Thankful Always   111

45. Deuteronomy 28: 1-14   113

46. Proverbs 27:17   116

47. Stinking Thinking   119

48. "Proof " Luke 2: 1-18   123

49. Creation   126

50. Fear Not !   127

51. Matthew 11:28   128

52. The 3D's.   130

53. Justified   132

54. The ABC's of Adversity   134

55. Healing   137

56. The Fall of Rome   138

57. The Greatest Gift Ever Given 141

58. Pray "God Sized" Prayers   144

59. Psalm 31:24   147

60. 1 John 4:4   149

61. Come As You Are   151

62. Winner's   153

63. Give Thanks   155

64. Finishing Grace   157

65. Run The Race To Finish   161

66. No Regrets   162

67. 1 Peter 5:8   164

68. 4 Steps Getting Back To God 166

69. Pray   168

70. What Does Your God Require Of You? 170

71. Praising God All Of The Time   171

72. 12 Ordinary Men   173

73. 7 Things God Detests   176

74. Who Is This Jesus?   177

75. Jesus Is The Same   181

76. Carry Your Own Cross   182

77. Praise God   183

78. Good News & Bad News   184

79. The Mustard Seed   190

80. God Hears Your Prayer   192

81. Psalm 55:22   194

82. Examine Yourself   195

83. John 3:16 The Gospel in 26 Words   199

84. Good Guys Finish 1st   204

85. Proverbs 3:5-6   205

86. The Psalms & James   206

87. End Times   208

88. James 1:2-4   210

89. Psalm 119:11   211

90. Trust In The Lord Believe In His Promises   213

91. 25 Bible Verses About Prayer   215

92. 20 Verses To Memorize   222

93. 43 Scriptures About Faith   226

94. Erie Invocation   234

95. The Glory And The Grace of God   235

96. The Valley Of Dry Bones   238

97. The Chain Breaker   240

98. The F.R.O.G. Concept   242

99. Jake Olsen   244

100. Great Moments With God   246

    About The Author   248

The Bible Explanation

God's greatest blessings come with an owner's manual.

The Bible contains the compassionate heart of God, the hopeless state of all mankind, the absolute, and only way of salvation. The Bible contains both the doom of doubters but also the complete happiness of His believers.

Its doctrines are holy, its precepts are binding, its histories are true, and its decisions are immutable. We read it to be wise, believe it to be safe, and when we obediently practice it, we become blessed beyond measure. It contains the light of the world to direct our every step, the bread of life to sustain us, the joy of the Lord to strengthen us and comfort to give us peace.

It is the traveler's map, the pilgrims' staff, the pilots compass, the soldier's sword, and the Christian's charter. In its pages Paradise is restored, Heaven opened, and the gates of Hell are sealed.

Christ is its grand subject, His will and our good design, and its inevitable end the greatest glory of God.

It should fill our thoughts and memories, rule our hearts, and guide our steps. Read it slowly, frequently, and prayerfully. It is more than a gold mine of wealth, a paradise of glory, and rivers of pleasure. It is given to us in life, it will be opened at the judgement, and the highest responsibility, will reward the greatest labor, but will condemn all who trifle with its sacred contents.

Read it and do what it says, because these pages contain exactly the reason why we were created They are the Holy Scriptures.

B - Basic

I - Instructions

B - Before

L - Leaving

E - Earth

Holy Bible Facts

There has been more archeological evidence, ancient manuscripts, and geopolitical discoveries supporting the Bible's validity than any other publication ever known to man.

1. More than 803,000 words

2. 27,000 verses

3. Over 3,600 unfailing promises of God.

4. 1,800 Chapters

5. 39 Old Testament books–written 1,600 years before Jesus.

6. 27 New Covenant books – written around the time of our Messiah's Birth, Ministry, Execution, and Resurrection. Son of God, Our Redeemer, JESUS.

7. 66 Books of the Bible

8. Translated and printed in over 2,400 languages with more copies printed and in use today NOT making it the bestselling book of the year, but the BESTSELLING BOOK OF ALL ETERNITY. IT IS…

THE BIBLE.

<u>3 Key Scriptures</u>:

- 2 Timothy 3:16

All Scripture is God breathed.

- 2 Peter 1:20

All prophecy comes from God

- Jeremiah 29:11

   For, I know the plans that I have for you; declares the LORD. Plans to prosper you and not harm you, plans for you to have Hope and a Future.

- The Validity of the bible:
  - Trust it, believe it, and live it!

  - God said it. You can believe it. And no one can dispute it.

- Never question the validity of the Word:

    - The Sword of the Spirit—the two edged sword

- Cling to the Belief:

"....it is WRITTEN".

Jesus rebuked Satan's temptation with these words;

"No man survives on bread alone, but by every word (that proceeds from the mouth of GOD)".
   I am GOD the SON

"You will worship GOD and serve Him only".
   I am GOD the SON

"You cannot tempt GOD."
   I am GOD the SON

John 8:32. If you know the Truth; the Truth will set you **FREE**.

The bible is more about Responsibilities than Rights

It's your compass through life;

It's your owner's manual to use in life's journey Jesus was asked more than once about the greatest commandments. And He replied, " *LOVE GOD, LOVE YOUR NEIGHBOR, AS YOURSELF, understanding that if you have little love for yourself, it will reflect poorly towards your neighbor as well.*
LOVE GOD as He is, was, and shall always be.
LOVE YOUR NEIGHBOR for he was created in the same fashion as you."

KNOW IT. PRACTICE IT.

SHOW IT.

THE NAME OF ABOVE ALL NAMES

God is revealed in His name!

1. **Elohim**: *Creator* (Genesis 1:1)
Referred to as the Creator more than any other name in the Hebrew with the understanding that prayers to the One that designed, constructed, built and orchestrates all that exists, could be the most trusted with our prayers.

2. **Adonai**: *Lord, Master* (Psalm 16:2)
As questionable as we have come to accept all authority on earth, it is important to remember, we are all a part of His plan, His authority, and His will. Irrespective of our circumstances, it is best to accept His invitation to follow Him, as it may be uncomfortable to be in His way. Submit to the will of the Master of all.

3. **Jehovah-M'Kaddesh**: *The God Who Sanctifies* (Leviticus 20:7-8)

Our God is uniquely Holy; extending His sanctification to all who place their faith in Him. This sanctification is only the beginning of a great transformation as you ask God to guide you and help you grow in this magnificent gift.

4. **Yahweh Roi**: *The Lord is My Shepherd* (Psalm 23:1-3)

A shepherd watches over his flock, but more so, protecting and caring for all those under His charge. He leads us beside still waters and lays in green pastures, because if we are not fed or watered, we don't sleep. He cares for his flock with no limitations to what he must sacrifice.

5. **El Roi:** *The God Who Sees* (Genesis 16:13-14)

Alone, forgotten, hurt or scared, call out to the God who sees you, no matter where you are or what you've done. When Hagar fled and God called to her in the wilderness, she called Him El Roi--that moment has felt so familiar to me many times.

6. **Yahweh Tsuri:** *The Lord My Rock* (Psalm 144:1)
When the entire foundations of the earth tremble, Yahweh Tsuri is unmovable and never changing. He is our firm foundation.

7. **Yahweh Nissi:** *The Lord My Banner* (Exodus 17:15-16)
The banner of the one we follow is also the values and practices that we also adhere to. This banner is what leads us to and victorious in every battle. The banner that we hold high and lifted up also identifies all of our resources guaranteeing the victory to our undeniable, undefeatable God. Stand confident that Yahweh Nissi is lifted over you. He is the strong and powerful battle cry of the victors.

8. **Jehovah Jireh:** *The God Who Provides* (Genesis 22:13-14)

> Abram clung for 100 years to God's promise of sons and daughters leaning solely on God's promise, so when his wish was granted only to require the death of his only heir, Abram could have had great difficulty being the obedient servant even to the point of denial, but his trust in God's Word placed him in a position that God could provide the alternative sacrificial ram.

9. **Jehovah Rophe:** *The God Who Heals* (Exodus 15:22-27)
Jehovah Goodwrench might imply that God can and does fix all things; body, mind, spirit or soul, however more than fixing, he heals all wounds completely beyond scars.

10. **Abba:** *Father* (Luke 15:20)
More than a positional relationship, ABBA would be more reminiscent a small child calling out "DADDY" to his (or her) unquestionable source of protection, provision, comfort, example and pinnacle of strength and righteousness, a loving father always near and always caring; an assurance of their place as a child and in the unconditional love of their parent. Rest in that relationship and love today.

Addendum

El: God (referencing might, power and strength of God, gods, or even men and angels.) El is
     almost always qualified by adding other names that distinguish GOD from false gods.

El Echad :*The One God.* (Mal 2:10)

El Hanne'eman: *The God that is Faithful (*Deut 7:9)

El Emet: *The God of Truth.*

"For You are my rock and my fortress…Into Your hand I commit my spirit; You have ransomed me, O Lord, God of truth."

Psalm 31:3 & 5

REMEMBER TODAY

Satan seeks to bring DEATH, DISEASE, DESTRUCTION, and SUFFERING TO ALL.

GOD never promised that there would never be difficult times ahead…

He promised that we would not have to face them alone.

God has been through everything that we could possibly imagine.

GOD gives us His STRENGTH to over-come it.

GOD has already defeated Satan at the empty grave…

TRUST HIM.

GOD'S ANSWERS TO SATAN'S LIES

1. Satan says: "It's impossible!"
GOD SAYS: "All things are Possible"
   Luke 18:27; Matt.19:26

2. Satan says: "You are too tired."
GOD SAYS: "I give you rest."
   Mathew 11:28-30

3. Satan says: "Nobody Loves you!"
GOD SAYS: "I love you."
   John 3:16;13:34

4. Satan says: "You can never go on."
GOD SAYS: "My Grace is sufficient for you". *II Cor. 12:9; Psalms 91:5*

5. Satan says: "You can never figure it out!"
*GOD SAYS:"I will direct your paths."*Prov 3:5-6

6. Satan says: "You can't do it!"
GOD SAYS: "You can do all things."   Phil. 4:13

7. Satan says: "You are not able."
  GOD SAYS: "I AM able."   II Cor.9:8

8. Satan says: "It's not worth it."
GOD SAYS:"It will be worth it." Romans 8:28

9. Satan says: "You can never forgive yourself."
GOD SAYS: 'I have FORGIVEN YOU."
   1 John 1-9; Romans 8:1

10. Satan says: "You can't manage
anything." *GOD SAYS: "I will supply all
your needs."* Phil. 4:9

11. Satan says: "You are a coward."
*GOD SAYS: "I have not given you a spirit of
FEAR."*   II Tim. 1:7

12. Satan says:"You will always be worried and frustrated".
GOD SAYS: "Cast all your cares on ME."
I Peter 5:7

13. Satan says: "You have no FAITH."
GOD SAYS:"I've given everyone a measure of FAITH." *Romans 12:3*

14. Satan says:"You are stupid."
GOD SAYS: "I give you Wisdom".
I Cor. 1:30

15. Satan says:"You are all alone".
GOD SAYS: "I will never leave you, nor forsake You." *Hebrews 13:5*

GOD SAYS:

"Jesus is the Same Yesterday, TODAY, and FOREVER."

Hebrews 13:8

LISTEN FOR GOD.

LISTEN TO GOD.

CHAPEL 6
PRAY

There are times when, weary of walking alone,
We need strength beyond our own.

Does a real man stand on his own two feet and rely on no one? **Only until he can't.** OR does he focus on the only One that can lift him up and wants to take him the distance.

Be thankful we serve a real God!

We were designed for relationship, not separation, but every time we pursue that independence, we will always fall short.

We were not designed to do it alone.

He makes a difference in your Life!

Simply ASK!

We serve a REAL GOD.Expect an answer.
" Ask, Seek and Knock and keep asking, seeking and knocking." (Matthew 7:7)

RIGHT EFFORT APPLIES to LIFE

KEEP IT R.E.A.L.

1. Keep it **Right**

2. Provide the **Effort**

3. **Apply** it to all situations

4. Make **Life** real.

Keep it REAL.

His ways are higher than our ways, but we only come to know His ways when we seek and make His ways our own.

Keep it REAL.

There is no path for fakes and pretenders.

Keep it REAL.

God's primary commandments that all other commandments are hinged on, "Love God with all you got,"and "Love your neighbor as yourself."

Keep it REAL.

God's love did not end on the Cross-it began there! He is alive and always ready to lift our heads and give us His glory.

Keep it REAL.

Our desire for every athletic team is to make their goal...

GET BETTER...
NOT BITTER!

The Power of Prayer

No ocean can hold it back.

No river can overtake it

No whirlwind can go faster

No army can defeat it

No law can stop it

No distance can slow it.

No disease can cripple it

No force on earth is more powerful or effective than the power of prayer!

"Pray continuously; give thanks in everything you do and in all circumstances." 1 Thessalonians 5:16

Always keep Praying. You have this great power- USE IT!

James 4:2

"You have not; because you ask not."

Above all - always keep praying!

God will not answer unspoken prayers.

-He knows all your needs before you ask

-**But** you must **ASK** and make your requests known to GOD; from you.

Remember *"You have not, because you ask not"*

• He wants you to **ASK!**

• Talk to God on a daily basis.

• Make your requests known to Him by faith with thanksgiving.

• Establish a Relationship with God; DAILY.

- Have faith and believe when you ASK.
- God will open the door when you KNOCK on it.

Pray continuously for all kinds of requests

"ASK AND YOU SHALL RECEIVE; SEEK AND YOU SHALL FIND; KNOCK AND THE DOOR SHALL BE OPENED."

Matthew 7:7

ASK,

SEEK,

KNOCK.

Whoever says,

"I don't
need God or
His prayers."

is a liar.

Pray for your PASTOR

10 Reasons to Pray without ceasing!

1. 1,500 pastors quit each month.

2. 7,000 churches close each year.

3. Only 10% of pastors – will retire from that position.

4. 70% of pastors ---battle depression.

5. 78% of pastors have no close friends.

6. 80% of pastors feel very discouraged or defeated.

7. 90% of pastors report working 55-75 hours per week.

8. 94% of pastors families feel pressure from the ministry.

9. 97% of pastors have been betrayed by friends and deeply hurt or falsely accused.

10. Please PRAY for your pastor today that God will lift him up!

3 Levels of PRAYER

Understanding effective PRAYER
Matthew 7:7

1. *Ask*, *and it will be given;*

2. *Seek*, *and you will find;*

3. *Knock*, *and it will be opened to you.*

It's as simple as English 101!
Pray :

NOUN.	A person, place, or thing
VERBS	An action
ADJECTIVE	Describes the noun
ADVERB	Modifies the action

Make your prayers specific, so that you may know God's will.

Do you know God's will?

- If we know HIS will in a matter—we ASK

- If we do not know His will –we SEEK

- If we know HIS will - but the answer has not come; we are to KNOCK until the door opens.

WHY CONTINUE TO KNOCK??
BECAUSE GOD SAID:

"Ask and it will be given to you; Seek and you will surely find it; Knock and the door will be opened to you".

Matthew 7:7

A.S.K.

"Ask and it will be given to you; Seek and you will surely find it; Knock and the door will be opened to you.".

Many believers NEVER get past the 1st level; they simply give up.

"...you have not because you ask not."

James 4:2

God does not answer *Unspoken Prayers*.

1. The 1st level of presenting a Petition: "Ask and it will be given to you"

   The verbs <u>ASK, SEEK,</u> and <u>KNOCK</u> simply means that the Subject is performing the action! (The action is ongoing).

   It's a command, it's not an option. ASK!

   --the promise of GOD is that they will receive [John 3:16 *"no one shall PERISH."*]

2. The level of pressing a PETITION.

   a. *"Seek, and you will find"*

   b. This is the action we take when we do not know the will of God but we seek until we find it --my input if you so choose to keep it.

   c. We will find out God's will for our lives; if we do not give up on seeking it.

   d. To Delay is not to Deny: Seek God's will for your life

3. The level persisting with a Petition.

   a. Knock and it will be opened to you

   b. Knocking involves tremendous perseverance

   c. Luke 11:5 tells us that

   d. We must keep on ASKING, SEEKING, and KNOCKING and hold to the promise that "It will be opened to you."

PUSH!

Pray Until Something Happens!

God knows what is best for us.

"Seek the face of God and HE will give you the Desires of your heart." Psalm 37:4

Persist in: ASKING, SEEKING, and KNOCKING

Never quit or give up; God will Honor your persistence!!

Different ways to PRAY:

1. Soaking prayer (constant prayer).

2. Specific time for prayer (morning, noon, or night).

3. Collective prayer (2 or more-group).

4. Specific purpose or subject (Special need).

5. Do not **Stop** till you hear from God.

6. Time elapsed –cannot be a factor.

7. Pray with your spouse or another Disciple of God with the same goal in mind.

Be ACCOUNTABLE: find a true prayer partner.

Commit to the Purpose or the need!

<u>5 Suggestions For A Great Prayer</u>

Always direct your prayer to the Holy Trinity!-Our
   sovereign God, the Father, the Son, and the Holy Spirit.

*Always offer to God the love and admonition due His
   Holy Name.*
> -Love Him; thank Him for your blessings!
> -Be thankful for what you have!

DO NOT DWELL ON WHAT YOU HAVE NOT!

Offer your prayer with great focus!
   -Offer your petition with gladness and
singleness of heart.
   -Pray with complete expectation that your
prayer will be answered.
   -Believe in your heart that God is listening.
    -Be very specific
   -Be patient and wait on God for your answer.
  Put no time limit on God's response to your
prayer.

-God responds in His time.

-Maybe God will decide not to answer your prayer immediately.

-If He never responds, it's because He has something better for you.

DESIGN YOUR PRAYER WITH GOD'S WORD IN IT!

-There are 43 scriptures found in God's word concerning prayer.

-Those scriptures tell us WHO, WHAT, WHERE, WHEN and WHY to pray.

(Find them highlighted in Chapel 91 of this book)

PUSH concept;

   Pray

   Until

   Something

   Happens

The Lord's Prayer

Not just church words.

The Lords Prayer is found in **Matthew 9:6.**

Jesus himself taught us how to pray.

- Think closely about its content.

- Jesus said; "this then is how you should pray".

LET'S BREAK THIS DOWN:

GOD said to HIS disciples:

This is how you should PRAY.

JESUS gave specific instructions and information teaching HIS disciples how to pray.

They will work for you!

Our FATHER which art in heaven; not just mine, yours, his, hers, or their father, but (OUR) father, making this (OUR) family calling upon our Holy Father ABBA, daddy, caring, protective strong yet compassionate. Far greater than anything on earth,

Hallowed be thy name; There is none like YOU…

Thy kingdom come, Thy will be

done on Earth, as it is in Heaven.

Give us this day our daily bread. Pray for provision. Daily bread refers to all we need to get by.

Forgive us our trespasses; as we FORGIVE those who trespass against us. Keep us from sinning and deliver us from the evil one. Forgive us for the sin that we commit daily. The prayer reminds us that we must forgive others.

Deliver us from the evil one;

For Thine is the Kingdom, the Power, and the Glory

Forever and ever. It also reminds us of God's great glory, forever.

AMEN

God makes it very clear that "This is how we should pray."

James Jones: A Great Success Story

A common name but an uncommon story. James Jones played for the Green Bay Packers as number 86- a Wide Receiver. James grew up homeless until the age of 16.

A great example of **Hard Work and Dedication-**

he never quit or gave up.

The family that never had anything:

❖ No father

❖ No money

❖ No clothes

❖ No food

❖ No home

❖ No car

❖ No measurable amount of anything

Park benches and homeless shelters were the only places he found to sleep or get food.

One day, he realized, his mom hadn't eaten in 4 days. He went into a pizza shop and begged the owner to give him a pizza, promising to pay him later.

After several hours; the owner agreed and James took the pizza to his mother.

After a second signing with Green Bay. (Yes, he was cut during his first year) he bought 2 homes! One for his mother and one for his own family.

It's not what you did or what happened to you;

it's what you do!!

EXAMPLE: when his friends went drinking; James Jones went to the gym to work out.

WHAT A SUCCESS STORY!!

Now a free agent ~~~~~~~~~~~~~~~~Again.

Don't give up on your dream and NEVER, NEVER, QUIT.

BY THE WAY: James went back and paid the owner of the pizza shop for the pizza; just like he said he would.
He kept his promise.

The Greatest Super Bowl Game EVER played!

The Greatest Super Bowl Game Ever Played!

It was Super Bowl LI (51). The Atlanta Falcons vs the New England Patriots played in Houston, Texas on February 5, 2017.

The following are factual events of the game:

1. 1st Super Bowl ever to go into OVERTIME.

2. Greatest deficit comeback in NFL history of any team.

3. Tom Brady engineered the comeback.

4. The 1st 3½ quarters belonged to the Atlanta Falcons.

5. The Falcons led the game 28-3.

6. The game was filled with bitter disappointments for the Patriots.

7. With 8 mins left in the 3rd quarter things began to drastically change.

8. It became a game of 30 minute halves.

9. The Falcons dominated the 1st 30 minutes but the Patriots dominated the 2nd half.

10. Tom Brady led his team to the greatest comeback in NFL history.

11. The only time the Patriots led in the game was the final play in overtime. Patriots won 34-28.

12. The way you handle adversity will determine your DESTINY.

13. Tom Brady finished the game with 466 yards. of offense.

14. A total Team VICTORY in attitude and effort.

15. Remember: **"It ain't over, till it's over."**

You can second guess the game all day long, but the Patriots found a way to WIN overcoming a 25 point deficit.

It is What It is!

Veterans Day

Take a moment to say to our men and women in uniform and those that have served in the past.

"We thank you for your service to our country".

We salute you for what you have done.

Your courage has kept us safe.

Your sacrifice has kept us free.

All of America owes you more than we can repay.

Please know that our thoughts and prayers are always with you.

We are the land of the free because of the **BRAVE.**

God Bless you always!

The Home of the FREE BECAUSE of the BRAVE!

Bible Emergency Numbers

We call emergency numbers to save us when we need help.

The Bible has them already programmed.
These Are More Effective Than 911!

These are direct lines. They are now and always open. **Call when....**

You are sad ...	John 14
You have sinned ...	Psalm 51
You are facing danger....	Psalm 91
People have failed you...	Psalm 27
It feels as though God is far from you......	Psalm 139
Your faith needs stimulation	Hebrews 11
You are alone and scared...	Psalm 23
You are worried...	Matt. 8:19-31

You are hurt and critical…	1 Corinthians 13
You wonder about Christianity…	2 Corinthians 5:15-18
You feel like an outcast…	Romans 8:31-39
You are seeking peace…	Matthew 11:25-30
It feels as if the world is bigger than GOD…	Psalm 93
You need Christ like insurance…	Romans 8:1-30
You are leaving home for a trip…	Psalm 121
You are praying for yourself…	Psalm 87
You require courage for a task…	Joshua 1
Finances are plaguing your thoughts…	Mark 10:17-31
You are depressed…	Psalm 27
You are broke…	Psalm 37

Mankind disappoints you..	1 Corinthians 13
People have been mean to you…..	John 15
You are losing hope…	Psalm 126
You feel small compared to the world…	Psalm19
You want to carry fruit…	John 13
Paul's secret for happiness…	Colossians 3:12-17
With big opportunity discovery…	Isaiah 55
To get along with other people…	Romans 12

*******ALTERNATE NUMBERS ******

For dealing with fear, call	Psalm 3:7
For security call	Psalm 12:1-3

| For assurance, call | Mark 8:35 |
| For reassurance, call | Psalm 145:18 |

All of these numbers may be dialed directly-

Operator assistance is not necessary!

FEED YOUR FAITH
AND YOUR DOUBT
WILL STARVE TO
DEATH!

GOD HONORS His Servants.

"The harvest is plentiful But the workers are few."

Matthew 9:37

God HONORS the person who SERVES. God LIFTS the person who is HUMBLE. GOD BLESSES the person who is FAITHFUL.

Do you want to know the SECRET formula for SUCCESS?

You must be willing to do the things that 99% of all people fail to do.

Practice, put in the time, putting, driving, sand traps, chipping, honesty, integrity, getting up early, work in the off season.

"The Lord makes firm the steps.

Of the one who delights in him:

Though he may stumble, he will not fail, for the LORD upholds him with his mighty hand.'

"THE HARVEST IS PLENTIFUL: BUT THE

LABORERS ARE FEW!"   *Matthew 9:37*

"TRUST IN THE LORD"

Proverbs 3:56

CHAPEL 20
THE 23RD PSALM

(More than just a child's memory verse)

The Twenty-Third Psalm

The LORD is my shepherd; I shall not want.

He maketh me to lie down in green pastures;

He leadeth me beside the still waters;

He restoreth my soul;

He leadeth me in the paths of righteousness for

His name's sake. …Yea, though I walk through

the Valley of the Shadow of Death, I will fear no

evil; for Thou art with me; Thy rod and Thy staff

they comfort me.

Thou preparest a table before me in the presence

of mine enemies; Thou anointest my head with

oil; my cup runneth over. Surely goodness and

mercy shall follow me all the days of my life;

and I will dwell in the house of the LORD forever.

NOT JUST CHURCH WORDS

The Lord is our Shepherd~

Isa 44:28; Ezek 34:11; Mica 5:4;

Hebrew 13:20; 1 Peter 5:4; Rev. 7:17

[metaphor Shepherd of ISRAEL]

Ezek 34:14&15 ; John 10:9

- We know his voice
- He heads the flock
- He finds lost sheep
- He protects them-not so with just a hired hand?
- **Lie Down:** Isa. 14:30; Ezek 34:11; Jer. 33:12; Zep. 2:7; 3:13
- **green pastures:** Contentment; Peace; provision
- **still waters**: safety, no danger; water substance of life

- **<u>Restores my Soul</u>** Restoration. Lam. 1:16; Prov. 25:13; Ruth 4:15

- In Him there is peace: no fear.

Righteousness:

Isa. 48:9&18; Prov. 8:20&21; 1 Kings 8:4; Jer. 14:21; Ezek. 20:9 & 14:22

- <u>paths of righteousness</u>: following in the footsteps of Jesus provides us the path of righteousness; Psalm 1-6; 34 &37

- <u>The way of the WICKED will</u> perish; Psalm 1

Valley of Shadow of Death: only the shadow of death remains. No more ambush only His favor.

I will fear no evil :even though it is around me. **Rod and Staff** : instruments of authority (Matt 28:20); fight off predators(Ex 21:20); protecting those who are out to get me (II Samuel 7:14)

Table Before Me: Celebration, banquet, food;

My cup runneth over: plentiful

Goodness and mercy: The righteous will prevail

Psalm 1: the wicked will perish ("Mercy is granted to those who fear God and ask for it"Matthew 7:7)

DWELL IN THE HOUSE OF THE LORD FOREVER: eternal life—future; Father's mansion has many rooms

God hears your Prayer!

He Knows, He Cares, He sees!

Talk to God every day! *And then listen…*

1. When God answers your prayers, **He increases your faith!**

2. When God delays, **He is increasing your patience in HIM.**

3. When God doesn't answer your prayer… He has something better for you. **So Trust Him.**

4. Thank God for His silence. **Something better is heading your way.**

"For I know the plans I have for you. Plans to prosper you and give you hope. Plans to give you a future."

Jeremiah 29:11

GOD WILL TAKE YOUR MESS; AND HE WILL TURN IT INTO YOUR MESSAGE!

One Solitary Life

"He was born in an obscure village
The child of a peasant woman
He grew up in another obscure village
Where he worked in a carpenter shop
Until he was Thirty years old
He never wrote a book
He never held an office
He never went to
college. He never
visited a large city
He never traveled more than 200 miles
From the place he was born
He did none of the things usually associated with
greatness
He had no credentials himself
He was 33 years old when he
died His friends ran away from
him
One of them denied him
He was turned over to his enemies

*And went through a mockery of a trial He
was nailed to a cross between two thieves
While dying, his executioners gambled for his
clothing
The only property he had on earth.
20 centuries have come and gone
And today Jesus is the central figure of the human
race
And the leader of mankind's progress
All the armies that have ever marched
All the navies that have ever sailed
All the parliaments that have ever sat
All the kings that have ever reigned put together
Have not affected the life of mankind on earth
As powerfully as that **ONE SOLITARY LIFE**."*

~Author: James Allan Frances,

1926~

When James Allan Frances penned that poem he wanted us to look at the simple life but powerful impact Jesus had on the world.

- One person made a difference

- Look ahead and count only on His direction.

- Understand that your salvation and future were predestined before the foundations of the Earth.

- God made us all DIFFERENT so that we each can make a difference.

CHAPEL 23
The Athlete's Prayer

Lord, clear my head of all distractions,

And my heart of burdens I bear

So I may perform my very best

Knowing You are always there.

With great courage I will meet this challenge,

As you would have me do

But keep me humble and remind me,

That my strength comes from You.

Then when all eyes are upon me,

At the end of the Big Game

I will turn their eyes to You O Lord

And to the Glory of Your Name.

Amen.

*Author Unknown

10
CHARACTER
TRAITS THAT
DAVID
MODELED
FOR US....

CHAPEL 24:
David: A man after God's own heart.

1. Devoted | Psalm 4:7

2. Recognized God | Psalm 9:1

3. Loving | Psalm 18:1

4. Reverent | Psalm 18:3

5. Trusting | Psalm 21:7

6. Continually Faithful | Psalm 23:6

7. Always Repentant | Psalm 25:1

8. Respectful | Psalm 31:39

9. Always Humble | Psalm 62:9

10. Obedient | Psalm 119:34

As we seek the attributes that earned David the title, "A man after God's own heart" we become "Men after God's own heart."

CHAPEL 25
God's Spoken Ministry

Dear Team;

I know each and every one of you better than you know yourselves right down to each hair on your head. I know the difficulties you have faced and the victories that you will achieve.

I know your hours of training and preparation. I know your physical condition and your mental state.

I know your personal struggles and those who depend on you. I know your medical condition and your financial struggles. I know your dreams and aspirations and I know the plans that I have for you are far greater than you could ever imagined. I know those who would try to stop you.

I also know that I love you and I will never leave you nor forsake you, and I am still on the throne...

Sincerely and eternally yours;

Abba Father

The Value of Hard Places

James 1:12. Trials

"Blessed is the man who remains steadfast while under trial; for when he has stood the test, he will receive the crown of life which God has promised to those who love him."

Isaiah 41:10

"Fear not, for I am with you; be not dismayed for I am your god; I will strengthen you, I will help you; I will uphold you with my righteous right hand."

Jeremiah 33:3

"Call on me and I will teach you great and unsearchable things you do not know."

The value of hard places:

We've all been there! Maybe you are there now! Hardships, uncertainty, difficulties that you cannot forget. No end in sight. No possible solution to your problem.

This is when we need God the most. This is when you get on your knees and ask the Father for Help.

1. Hard places teach us to **Pray**. We need God's help. **Now!**

2. Hard places make **Christ** real. We cry out for help and solutions to a higher power.

3. Hard places teach us **Patience**. Patience teaches us perseverance.

4. **PUSH-**Pray until something happens.*(Pg.46)*

5. Hard places teach us **Courage.** We learn to rely on God's Grace during our suffering. We must have Hope in God.

6. Hard places provide us with **Faith.** It teaches us to believe and trust in God. No matter what the circumstances might be!

7. Hard places teach us to help others in similar situations. Your experiences can council others in their time of need.

REMEMBER :

PROVERBS 3:5-6

"Trust in the Lord with all your heart; lean not on your own understanding.

In all your ways acknowledge Him and He will make your paths straight."

Trade "I Can't" For-
"I CAN, I WILL, I DID!"

Prayer is the Key to Heaven but Faith unlocks the door!

The Priestly Blessing

"And the Lord said to Moses. Tell Aaron and his sons. This is how you should bless the Israelites; say to them;

The Lord bless you and keep you.

The Lord make His face to shine upon you, and be gracious unto you.

The Lord turn His face toward you and give you peace."

Numbers 6:22-26

*May the Peace that passes all human understanding be with all of you, now and forever.

1 THESSALONIANS 1:2&3

FAITH, LOVE & HOPE

"WE ALWAYS THANK GOD FOR ALL OF YOU, MENTIONING YOU IN OUR PRAYERS. WE CONTINUALLY REMEMBER YOU BEFORE OUR GOD AND FATHER."   1 Thessalonians 1:2-3

1. YOUR WORK PRODUCED BY FAITH.

2. YOUR LABOR PROMPTED BY LOVE.

3. YOUR ENDURANCE INSPIRED BY HOPE IN OUR LORD JESUS CHRIST.

The Way To Live Your Life

1. DO WHAT IS RIGHT

2. DO YOUR VERY BEST

3. TREAT OTHER PEOPLE THE WAY YOU WOULD LIKE TO BE TREATED

4. KNOW THAT YOU REALLY MAKE A DIFFERENCE

5. TALK WITH GOD, PRAISE HIM, LISTEN TO HIM, OBEY HIM, ALLOW HIM TO BLESS YOU.

6. FOR YOUR FAMILY, FRIENDS, TEAM, OR BUSINESS

"Call to me and I will answer you and tell you great and unsearchable things you do not know." Jeremiah.33:3

"Give thanks to the Lord God Almighty for the Lord is good, His Love Endures Forever."

Things You Can Control

1. Attitude

2. Effort

3. Enthusiasm

These are the only factors that you can really control; so concentrate—only on them for your game preparation.

REMEMBER: Nothing else matters!

~What your opponents do…doesn't matter!

~What the media says….doesn't matter!

~What the critics say….doesn't matter!

-What your fans think….doesn't matter!

~What the odds are….doesn't matter!

Nothing else matters; except what the coaches and players think.

CHAPEL 31
What You Believe Is Critical

If you think you can...
    YOU WILL!
If you think you can't...
    YOU'RE ABSOLUTELY RIGHT!

Many players become distracted by other things which they cannot control.

Focus only on the fundamentals which you can control.

If you do that, it will put you in the driver's seat-totally in charge of your own **DESTINY.**

The same applies to the life of a Christian:
1. Always trust God.

2. Make time for God's Word, DAILY.

3. Pray on all occasions with EVERY request, and all praise and worship. Thank Him for all of your victories, past, present and future.

Never cease these things, drawing nearer to Him, and He draws near to you.

The way that you handle your adversity will determine your Destiny.

God is in control, and wants to trade your adversities for His victories.

Trust in Him.
Always.

7 Ways To Become A Godly Man

How to be a Godly Person:

1. ***Put God first*** *in everything you do.*
   Your Work, play, leisure, and life Ask God if it's where He wants you to be.

2. *Always* ***do what's right.***

   Not what you think that you can get away with, or what your peers tell you to do. Not what the majority may be doing. Always make the right choice, even when it's tough.

3. *Always use your* ***wisdom.***

   The Bible tells us that there are 2 kinds of wisdom. That which comes from the knowledge of books and that wisdom which comes from on high. Rely on God's wisdom. Fear the Lord is the first sign of wisdom.

4. *Always be* **responsible.**

Take responsibility for all that you do, good and bad. Never evade it!

5. *Always be* **honest.**

From God no secrets are hid! He knows everything present, past, and future.

6. *Always have* **courage.**

Like Paul, never give up and always keep pressing on toward the goal. Never quit. Perseverance must always be completed to make you become whole.

7. *Always display the* **Compassion of Jesus.**

You (must) forgive others; so that the Father in Heaven will forgive you.

CHAPEL 33
You Were Created To Serve Others

Develop the habit to serve God in all that you do.

Don't expect to get paid for it or expect to get something back in return.

REMEMBER:

Put God's Word in your mind when you don't need Him and God's Word will be there, when you do need it.

We were created by God to serve others.

God will recharge your life; when you lift others in need.

Encourage others to trust in God.

Look for ways to help others in need.

Kind words work wonders.

Serve the ones you love the MOST.

** Jesus washed the disciple's feet to show how He served.

Serve someone today besides yourself.

Scripture says: NEVER get tired of doing the right thing.

God will see what you are doing and great is your reward.

Help someone else to reach their dreams, goals, and ambitions.

God is counting on you to do it **TODAY!!!!**

Give back to people; in some way **TODAY!!!!**

When you bless others; God blesses you.

"It's always better to give, than to receive."

Don't Quit Poem

"When things go wrong as they sometimes will.
When the road you're trudging seems all uphill
When the funds are low and the debts are high
And you want to smile, but you have to sigh,
When care is pressing you down a bit
Rest if you must but don't you quit

Life is queer with it's twists and turns
As everyone of us sometimes learns,
And many a failure turns about
When he might have won had he stuck it out
Don't give up though the pace seems slow
You may succeed with another blow

Often the goal is nearer than
It seems to appear to a faltering man
Often the struggler has given up
When he might have captured the victor's cup
And he learned too late when the night slipped
down

How close he was to the golden crown.

Success is a failure turned inside out
The silver tint of clouds of doubt
And you never can tell how close you are
It may be near when you seem so far
So stick to the fight when you are hardest hit
It's when things seem worst, you must not quit."

- Anonymous

TEAm Work will make The Dream Work!

CHAPEL 35

10 Things God Wants You To Remember

1. I will give you rest. Lam 5:5

2. I will strengthen you. Psalm 18:32

3. I will answer you. Luke 7:18

4. I believe in you. John 17:6

5. I will bless you. Psalm 68:9

6. I am for you. II Cor 4:16

7. I will not fail you. Hebrews 13:5

8. I will provide for you. Psalm 37:18

9. I will be with you. Hebrews 13:8

10. I love you. John 3:16

SIMPLE TRUTHS:
A way to lead your life-

1. Always do what is **RIGHT.**

2. Always do your very **BEST**.

3. Always **TREAT** others as you would appreciate being treated.

The Christian Warrior
EPHESIANS 6:10-19

ARMOR OF GOD
EPHESIANS 6:10-18

The Helmet of Salvation
Put on the Helmet of Salvation by believing that Jesus Christ died for your sins and rose again.

The Breastplate of Righteousness
Righteousness is being honest, good, humble and fair to others. It means standing up for weaker people.

The Shield of Faith
Faith is being sure that God will keep His promises. Faith in God protects you when you are tempted to doubt.

The Belt of Truth
Truth keeps us from giving in to world's beliefs. Compare your beliefs and action to the truth of the Word of God.

Feet Prepared with the Gospel of Peace
The Gospel of Peace is being right with God and being contented in troubled times. Jesus said, peacemakers were blessed.

The Sword of the Spirit
which is the Word of God. God's Word is our offensive weapon. When we tell others about the Bible says, the Holy Spirit helps people see their bad thoughts and actions, and makes them want to be forgiven.

UNDER HIS WINGS

"As the eagle must force her young

from the nest to teach them how to <u>fly</u>,

So our <u>Father</u> must press us out of routine

To the things He'd have us <u>try</u>…

And just as the eagle guards her own

to insure their safety in <u>flight</u>,

Our Lord is near when we try our wings.

We're <u>never</u> out of His sight……

But should the eaglet begin to fall,

the eagle swoops down from <u>above</u>

To rescue its young and bear it up

on <u>wings</u> of strength and <u>love</u>

So how can we doubt that the eagles Creator,

the One Who made us <u>all</u>

Would fail to save and deliver us,

if <u>we</u> should start to <u>fall</u>?" Author B.J. Hoff

Never Say Never

"Nothing is impossible with God." Luke 1:37
"Everything is possible."   Matt 19:26

"The Lord gives strength to the weary and increases the power of the weak." Isa 40:29

"I can do everything through Christ who gives me strength." Philippians 4:13

"Now what I am commanding you today is not too diffi-cult for you or beyond your reach." Deuteronomy 30:11

"Commit to the Lord whatever you do and your plans will succeed." Proverbs 16:3

"If you believe, you will receive whatever you ask for in prayer." Matthew 21:22

Beyond the matter of "seeing is believing",
BELIEVING IS SEEING...

Mother's Day

M is for the million things she gave me,

O means only that she's growing old,

T is for the tears she shed to save me,

H is for her heart of purest gold;

E is for her eyes, with love-light shining,

R means right, and right she'll always be,

Put them all together, they spell

"MOTHER", a word that means the world to me.

-Anonymous

Praising God

ALL THE TIME!

The deepest level of worship is praising God in spite of the pain that you are experiencing;

Thank God during your trial.

Trust Him when you are tempted to lose hope.

Love Him, even when He seems so distant and so far away.

At my lowest, God is my Hope;

At my darkest, God is my Light;

At my weakest, God is my Strength;

At my saddest, God is my Comforter.

Thank you, Jesus for loving me, just the way I am.

Amen

Sanctification

The book of Romans, chapter 8 has been considered

"The diamond ring of the Bible."

"The sparkle of the diamond."

THE HOLY SPIRIT:

The creative power of God.

Is the resurrection power of God.

Is the indwelling power of God.

Is our teacher.

Is our counselor.

Is our intercessor.

Is our Giver of Gifts.

Is our Giver of Peace, Joy, and Wisdom.

The 3 fold nature of man:

1. The body of man. (senses)

2. The soul of man. We are born in a sinful nature.

3. The spiritual nature of man. God is Within us.

   a. Sin is still within us;

   b. Practice does not make perfect.

   c. Practice makes habitual—do it enough times and get it right.

A habit takes 21 days in a row to form or break.

Get in the habit of doing things **RIGHT** OR

Develop the habit of doing things **WRONG.**

Either way; you will develop a **HABIT.**

It's your choice!

"THERE IS THEREFORE, NOW NO CONDEMNATION FOR THOSE WHO ARE IN CHRIST JESUS." Romans 8:11

SIN

Sin leads to shame

Shame leads to guilt, and guilt leads to condemnation in our souls. (It can be a painful process in our lives.)

The Spirit bears witness with our spirit for the Lord Jesus Christ,.

The Spirit intercedes for us (Pray in the spirit with groanings)

The Gospel (Good News) helps us to live in the Spirit; Free of Sin, if we so choose.

Know and follow the Word of God .

****Meditate on it*****

"I have hidden your word in my heart; so that I might NOT sin against you, oh, Lord."

~Psalm 119:11

John's Gospel (Who Jesus Is)

Who Jesus is!

If you haven't started reading God's word yet, one of the best places to start is the Gospel of John to find out about Jesus!

You can start with the most quoted verse in the bible: John 3;16. This scripture explains the Gospel in 26 words.

However there is much more:

1. **John 3:16**, tells the complete story of the Gospel in 26 words.

2. **John 14:13,14**   The drinking of the. water.

3. **John 6:35**, I am the Bread of Life.

4. **John 8:12**, I am the Light of the World.

5. **John 10:9**, I am the Door.

6. **John 10:11**, I am the Good Shepherd.

7. **John 11:25**, I am the Resurrection and the Life.

8. **John14:6**, I am the Way, the Truth, and the Life.

9. **John 15:1**, I am the True Vine.

10. **John 11:43**; Lazarus-come Forth.

11. **John 11:44**, Loose him and let him go!

12. **John 8:32**, You shall know the Truth, and the Truth shall set you Free.

13. **John 7:37**, If any of you **Thirst**, let him come to me and **Drink**.

John's Gospel
"IT IS FINISHED"

What does "It is Finished" mean?

1. It is Finished means—my debt is paid.

2. It is Finished means—the battle is over.

3. It is Finished means—there is no more War.

4. It is Finished means—the end of Conflict.

Jesus is Lord.

- All scripture concerning Christ suffering were fulfilled. **Isaiah 53**.

- Satan was defeated. **John 12:31-33.**

- The middle wall of partition separating Jews and Gentiles was split. **Romans 10:11 &12; Ephesians 2:14-18.**

- We now have access to the throne of God. **Hebrews 10:16 &19.**

- The reign of death is cancelled. **Romans 5:12-21**
- The power of sin was broken.**Romans 6**

- Salvation from sin-any and all sin. **Hebrews 9:11-14.**
- Peace between God and man was restored. **Romans 5:1-11.**

- The justice of God was satisfied. **Romans 3:21-26.**

- Healing for the body, soul and mind. **Isaiah 53:4 & 5.**

- The indwelling of the Holy Spirit in God's people. **Acts 1:4-8**.

It is finished! Never again will Christ have to come to die on the cross.

AMEN!

Less Is NOT More

Welcome to the 21st Century.

Our phone-*wireless*

Cooking-*fireless*

Cars-*keyless*

Food-*fatless*

Tires-*tubeless*

Dress-*sleeveless*

Youth-j*obless*

Leaders-*shameless*

Relationships-*meaningless*

Attitude-*careless*

Wives-*fearless*

Babies-*fatherless*

Feelings-*heartless*

Education-*valueless*

Children-*mannerless*

Society-*thoughtless*

Everything is becoming LESS but still our hopes are- **Endless.**

In fact we are –*Speechless.* And Congress is- *Clueless.*

Sometimes our favorite football team is *Winless!*

The more we use God's word in our lives, the more we keep the devil out of our lives!

Be Thankful Always

Be Thankful Always!

Jehovah Jireh, God provider, makes certain that we have all that we need to Glorify His Name and bring our praises to Him only.

IT WOULD CERTAINLY BE NICE TO BE PERFECTLY HEALTHY, with NICE CLOTHING, a NICE HOME, NICE FOOD...

Wouldn't everything be NICE?

Be Thankful Always!

Whatever it is in your life that God has blessed you with; recognize that God has given it to you, with His unlimited grace and power for His Glory.

BE THANKFUL ALWAYS!

But one day it can all be taken from you.

BE THANKFUL ALWAYS!

Sometimes things get in the way, and our praises stop going up… Sometimes we need reminded, that the greatest blessing that we could ever receive, is a loving and caring Father in Heaven when our eyes are more focused on our surroundings instead of Him.

OUR GOD IS ALWAYS ABLE.

Deuteronomy 28:1-14

The Blessing of God for Obedience.

1. Obey the Lord in all things.

2. Obey the Lord and he will give you Provision.

3. You will be blessed.

4. Everything you have will be blessed by God.

5. Your needs will be met with favor.

6. You will be blessed at all times.

7. Your enemies will be defeated.

8. God will bless you.

9. Keep the commands of the Lord.

10. The world will see that you belong to the Lord.

"Humble yourselves, therefore, under God's mighty hand, that He may lift you up in due time." **1 Peter 5:6**

"I call on the Lord in my distress, and He answers me."
Psalm 120:1

We serve a living GOD who loves us all unconditionally and will keep us in His favor!

The LORD will NEVER let us down.

"Jesus Christ is the same yesterday, today, and forever."
Hebrews 13:8

"May the God of Hope fill you with Joy and Peace as you Trust in Him, so that you may over-flow with Hope by the Power of the Holy Spirit."

Romans 15:13

GOD IS FAITH, HOPE, AND LOVE.

We must understand that!

1 Thessalonians 1:2 is Paul writing to the Thessalonians.

We always give thanks for you remembering you in our prayers; for

❖ Work produced by Faith

❖ Labor prompted by Love
❖ Hope inspired by the Holy Spirit. Let the words of Paul in this letter to the Thessalonians be a constant inspiration to you.

Proverbs 27:17

"As iron sharpens iron; so one person sharpens another."

Great people on a good team, make everyone else around them a better player.

That is why we always need a great leader among us.

A great leader inspires everyone among us.

A great leader lifts everyone to become stronger as a performer and to always get better.

On any team "it's not the size of the dog in the fight; but it's the size of the fight in the dog."

Teammates must always pull together despite the level of adversity that they face together.

On any Athletic Team it is a fact of life that at some point, you will face adversity, or some kind of trial.

HOW WILL YOU REACT TO IT?

In 2016, the Cleveland Cavaliers were down in the NBA finals three games to one. No team in the NBA had ever overcame a deficit like that.

Because the team pulled together, the Cavs became the 2016 World Champions! By not listening to doubters and believing in themselves, they controlled their own destiny. That made the comeback sweeter!

The way you handle the situation will determine your personal level of **SUCCESS.**

Carefully pick the people with which you associate or surround yourself.

Always remember that **"Iron Sharpens Iron"**.

"It's not how many times you get knocked down. It's how many times you get back up!"

Work your hardest to become that **great one** on your team.

Be that army of one; and it will lead you to **SUCCESS.**

Say the Lord's Prayer.

Stinking Thinking*

1. I'll never accomplish my dreams. I do not have what it takes.

   "The favor of the Lord rests on me and makes my efforts successful." **Psalm 90:17**

2. I'm not talented.

   "God has given me Special Gifts, and I'm going to share them with others." **1 Peter 4:10**

3. I'll never break this addiction.

   "I can do anything through Christ who strengthens me." **Philippians 4:3**

4. Nothing good is in my future. *"God knows the plans He has for me – good plans to give me a hopeful future."* **Jeremiah 29:11**

5. I'm not attractive or good enough.

   "I am fearfully and wonderfully made by Almighty God, and His works are wonderful." **Psalm 139:14.**

6. I'll never get out of here.

   "God opens doors in my life that; no one can shut." **Revelation 3:8**

7. I have no money!

   "God will supply my every need; according to His riches in Glory. **Philippians 4:19**

8. My life is a series of unfortunate events.

   "No weapon turned against me will ever succeed. Every voice that raises up against me, will be silenced." **Isiah 54:17**

9. I'll never be able to come out on top.

"God has made me the head, not the tail. With Him, I am always at the top, never on the bottom. **Deuteronomy 28:13**

10. I can't stop worrying.

"I'm not anxious about anything. My heart's not troubled, for God has given me peace. **Philippians 4:6; John 14:27**

11. I'm getting old and tired.

"I trust in the Lord and have fresh strength. I soar like an eagle through life. I'm not weary or faint. **Isaiah 40:31**

12. No one cares about me.

"The Lord is mindful of me. I am so valuable to Him. **Psalm 115:12 Matthew 10:31**

13. I have no hope of ever getting well.

"Because of what Jesus did on the Cross for me; I am healed. **Isaiah 53:5**

14. I am completely stressed out.

"No worries, God's peace guards my heart and mind. He takes care of me. **Philippians 4:7; Psalm 52:22**

*Trinity Broadcasting Network.

God truly wants

YOU

to succeed!

Let Him help YOU do

that today!

"PROOF" Luke 2:1-18

Some people believe that Jesus is a myth. The Bible is a historical document that proves otherwise:

Luke 2:1-18

Jesus' birth was proven by history;

Luke 2:1-7. Caesar Augustus called for a census so he could collect taxes.

City of Bethlehem; Jesus was born.

Jesus' birth was proclaimed by Heaven.

Luke 2:8-14

Showed the Glory of the Lord

Good news/Bad news—

Romans 6:23 *"All have sinned and fallen short of the Glory of God."*

"The wages of Sin is Death".

The host angel told of the joy that was gained when Christ was born.

Angels chanted together;

"HOLY, HOLY LORD; GOD OF POWER AND MIGHT; HEAVEN AND EARTH ARE FULL OF YOUR GLORY."

Good news and great joy was proclaimed!

The Son and Savior of Almighty God is documented.

He is REAL!

Jesus is the Word.

John 1:1-2

Creation

God delivered his people from Egypt.

Genesis 1:1-3

God is personally involved with all creation.
God created by his spoken word..
Romans 1:16 God said…*"And it was so."*
6 days of work and 1 day of rest.

God is more concerned about your character,
than your conduct.

Genesis 3. Adam and Eve. Sin entered in.

Romans 5:17… God's free gift of righteousness.

Genesis 3:8 "…They hid from God because of
their Sin."

**We serve a God of wonders: Lord of All Creation…
Believe it!**

God is ABLE and WILLING!

Thanks be to God Almighty!

Fear NOT!

"FEAR NOT, FOR I AM WITH YOU: DO NOT BE DISMAYED, FOR I AM YOUR GOD. I WILL STRENGTHEN YOU. I WILL UPHOLD YOU WITH MY RIGHTEOUS RIGHT HAND."

ISAIAH 41:10

God will strengthen you!

❖ God will help you in all situations (if you just **ASK**). **Matthew 7:7**.

❖ We have a loving God who cares for us.

❖ Fear not, means what it says-DO NOT HAVE FEAR!

❖ God is always with us and hears our requests and He knows our hearts.

Matthew 11:28

SEEK GOD'S FACE.

SEEK GOD'S DIRECTION.

SEEK GOD'S WILL.

SEEK GOD'S STRENGTH.

SEEK GOD'S REST.

It would concern me if anyone other than Jesus had extended this invitation.

"For my yoke is easy; and my burden is light."

Matthew 11:30

God knows our capabilities as we are, and what we can accomplish. God knows ALL THINGS, even what He can accomplish in our lives, and through us.

We will achieve all that God has planned for us when we first seek His face…

"COME TO ME ALL WHO ARE WEARY AND HEAVY-LADEN, AND I WILL GIVE YOU REST. TAKE MY YOKE UPON YOU AND LEARN FROM ME, FOR I AM GENTLE AND HUMBLE IN HEART , AND YOU WILL F I N D R E S T F O R Y O U R SOULS. FOR MY YOKE IS EASY AND MY BURDEN IS LIGHT".

MATTHEW 11:28-30

The 3 D's

The 3 D's of sports:
Desire.
Determination.
Dedication

The 3 D's of GOD:

❖ **Discover**. Find out more about the living God. *(Read the Word)*

Discover

Develop

Deploy

❖**Develop.** Find out about what God has called us to do for Him. *(Understand the Word)*.

- ❖ **Deploy.** Put it into action (do the things that God has commanded us to do. (Carry out the Word).

"God is unchangeable, unstoppable and always the same yesterday, today, and forever! "

John 13: 1-17; 31-35

Jesus washes the feet of His disciples.

It teaches us:

   - to serve one another with **HUMILITY.**

   - Jesus washed their feet and used the apron and the towel, in **HUMILITY.**

   - Jesus told us to "love one another as I have loved you". Serve with **HUMILITY.**

Justified

Justified (Just as if I'd never SINNED)

Romans 5:

Vs 1. Peace with God   **HOSTILE**
Vs 2. Access to God   **HAUGHTY**
Vs 4. Hope to God   **HELPLESS**
Vs 5. God poured out His love and grace to all of us.
       ABUNDANCE
Vs 8. Christ died for all of us while we were still sinners. **Greater Love has no man.**

Communion – *a reminder to us about God's unconditional love for us.*

Broadness of Justification.

Romans 5:11 tells us:

- Joy for forgiveness of ALL our **SINS.**
       ALL IS FORGIVEN

- God makes us all INNOCENT of our past sins; **FORGIVENESS IS YOURS FOR THE ASKING!**

MATTHEW 7:7 ASK

Romans 5:1 Therefore means: that's what it's there for.

FORGIVENESS: IT'S A FREE GIFT FROM GOD; ALL WE HAVE TO DO IS ASK FOR IT!

The ABC's Of Adversity

"If you faint in the day of adversity; your strength is small." **Proverbs 24:10**

Walt Disney said: *"All the adversity in my life; all my troubles and obstacles have really strengthened me!"*

❖ The strengthening power of ADVERSITY is true.

❖ Teams can't win; without opposition.

❖ Wisdom isn't gained without mistakes.

❖ Leaders don't rise to greatness without crisis and tough times.

❖ ADVERSITY builds emotional muscle and creates reliable leaders that prepare us for difficult situations.

❖ Adversity will prepare us for great things.

REMEMBER the ABC's of Adversity:

ADVERSITY

BUILDS

CHARACTER

The Lord draws near to us in tough times and helps us to Trust Him in times of difficulty.

We need to know:

❖ Tough times don't last.

❖ Tough people do.

Rely on God for all your needs; and Trust Him especially, when times get difficult.

When things are
going great:
Praise His name.

When things are
getting really tough:
Do the same!
AMEN

Healing

Anoint with blessed oil and call the Elders together for the laying on of hands and prayer.

When we are **FAITHLESS,**

God is always **FAITHFUL!!**

James 5:14-15 (KJV)

> *Is any sick among you? let him call for the elders of the church; and let them pray over him, anointing him with oil in the name of the Lord:*

> *And the prayer of faith shall save the sick, and the Lord shall raise him up; and if he has committed sins, they shall be forgiven him.*

Mark 6:13. *Pray in the Spirit! God will intercede for us in prayer.*

The Fall Of Rome

The greatest nation in the history of the world self-destructed because;

- *God's work was denied or deferred.*

- *God's worship was diverted or decayed.*

- *God's presence was forbidden or forgotten*

We are to be in the world but NOT of the world, Jesus said

These were the reasons that Rome self-destructed...

- Righteous values of marriage, family and sanctity of the home were replaced with pride, lust, and greed.

- Craze for pleasure: Sports, sex & drugs overshadowed the religious fibers that held family and society together.

- Redistribution of wealth (increased taxation in spite of the state of the union).

- Constant wars (Man will self-destruct).

- Decay of Religion. (No church, no marriage values).

- Elimination of God in their everyday lives.

- Man becomes his own god. (No bible, no church, divorce 50%)

- They were destroyed from within. (Self-destruction from the inside is what caused Rome to crumble.).

The greatest nation in the history of the world, completely destroyed itself from within…

Does any of this sound familiar?

Jesus said: *"My kingdom is not of this world. You can't love me and the world together. "* One or the other.

America is headed for self-destruction from within.

Where do you stand??

Is God a vital part of your life?

Are you serving Him or are you too busy?

What other God's are you worshipping? (technology, etc).

GOD THE FATHER, GOD THE SON, AND GOD THE HOLY SPIRIT IS THE ONLY TRUE GOD IN THIS WORLD.

The Greatest Gift Ever Given

Did you get the Gift you always wanted?

When you opened the Gift were you overjoyed?

How has God Blessed you?

- Intelligence
- Athletic ability
- Charitable giving
- A wonderful family
- A child or children
- A special talent
- A sense of determination
- A heart for Him (The Lord)

Do you have?

Love, Joy, Peace, Happiness, Gentleness, Kindness, Forbearance, Goodness, Faithfulness, and Self-control.

These are the Fruit of the Spirit found in **Galatians 5:22.**

A Christian life produces such things.

However, in the Gospel of John Chapter 1, we find God's greatest Gift of all.

John 1:1-4: *"In the beginning was the Word, the Word was God and the Word was with God; In the beginning through Him, all things were made."*

John 1:14: *"The Word became flesh and dwelt among us. We have seen His glory, the glory of the one and only Son of God, who came from the Father, full of grace and truth."*

God sent His only Son to us to die on the cross for the Atonement of our Sins.

This is the Greatest Gift that we could ever receive!

John 3:16: The most quoted verse in the bible--- *"For God so loved the world that He gave His only begotten son, that whosoever shall believe in Him, should not perish but have ever-lasting life."*

Pray "God-sized" Prayers

"You have not, because you ask not."

James 4:2-3

If you pray for small things, that's good, but you only get small things in return.

Pray God-sized prayers, for the desires of your heart. Ask BIG and receive BIG!

Do not limit God but challenge God.

Don't pray safe prayers. Pray faith prayers. Know that God will hear you and answer you.

(If you have been faithful to Him). God will take you to places that you never dreamed of going!

Never give up on your prayer! Speak it into existence!

Take the limits off of Almighty God.

He created the world and everything there-in. **God can and does, work MIRACLES today!**

Be **BOLD** in your prayers; and God will be **BOLD** in His answers!

Pray and believe and you will receive.

God will turn your **MESS** into your message.

He will make your **TEST** into your Testimony.

TRUST AND OBEY HIM EVERYDAY!

Psalm 31:24

"Be of good courage, and He will strengthen your heart, all of you that hope in the Lord."

God will give you the desires of your heart if you are **RIGHTEOUS** in His sight and seek Him.

You must follow Him and truly walk the talk!

If you have a cross around your neck, but you don't have Jesus in your HEART, then you are wasting your time & your religion is worthless.

Remember: from God, *no secrets are hid.*

He knows, He cares and He sees, everything you think, say and do. *Think about that!*

What a mighty God we serve!

CHAPEL 60

1 John 4:4

"GREATER IS HE THAT IS WITHIN ME; THAN HE THAT IS IN THE WORLD."

Romans 8:1, *"There is therefore, now no condemnation to those who are in Christ Jesus."*

II Corinthians 5:7, *"I walk by faith and not by sight."*

Isaiah 65:24, *"You declared that before I called; You would answer, and while I was yet speaking, You would hear."*

Romans 8:28, *"Father, I am called according to Your purpose, and therefore I rejoice that all things will work together for good, because I love God."*

Proverbs 18:10, *"I thank You today that Your Name is a strong tower. The righteous run into it and are safe."*

Philippians 4:13, *"I can do all things through Christ who strengthens me."*

Psalm 27:1, *"Father, You are my light and my salvation. Whom shall I fear? You are the strength of my life; of whom shall I be afraid?"*

THE
CHOICE
IS YOURS!

CHAPEL 61

Come As You Are!

Colossians 3:17 & 23

"And whatsoever ye do in word or deed, do all in the name of the Lord Jesus, giving thanks to God and the Father."

"And whatsoever ye do, do it heartily, as to the Lord, and not unto men;"

Hold on to God and He will hold onto you.

The Testimony comes only after the test

Life will always give us adversity; *so keep your focus on God.* God will make a way when there seems to be no way.How we handle our adversity will determine our destiny!

God will deliver you, *if* you seek Him with a just heart. God will *never* give up on you or let you down.

When things are going good **"Praise His name."**

When things are getting tough, **"Do the same."**

God will take your mess and make it your message in **VICTORY!**

Always remember that,

"Tough times don't last; tough people do!"

Trust in God and seek His face with *everything* you do in life and He will give you the desires of your heart!!

A great promise of God.

"The great promise of God, I will never leave you; nor forsake you." **Hebrews 13:5**

Winners

Winners are people just like you.

- Winners take chances. Like everyone else they fear failing, but they refuse to let fear control them.

- We know that tough times never last; tough people do.

- Winners don't give up; when life gets rough they hang in there, until the going gets better.

- Winners are flexible. They realize there is more than one way and are willing to try others.

- Winners know they are not perfect. They respect their weaknesses while making the most of their strengths.

- Winners fall *but they don't stay down.* They stubbornly refuse to let failure keep them from climbing. Winners don't blame fate for their failures nor luck for their successes.

Winners accept responsibility for their lives and performances

- Winners are positive thinkers who see the good in all things; from the ordinary to the extraordinary.

- Winners FOCUS on their path ahead of them even when they stumble, they get back up Even when others can't see your destination, You press on.

- Winners are patient. They know how important it is and keep their eye on the prize.

- Winners are willing to do the difficult things striving for SUCCESS.

- Winners go the distance knowing that their efforts make the world a much better place to be.

Philippians 4:13, *"I can do all things through Christ who strengthens me."*

Give Thanks

Give thanks: for His steadfast love endures forever!

Read **Psalm 136:1-26**

> Give thanks to God for His love.

- ◆ The Lord....   *Jehovah*

- ◆ The God of God's... *Elohim*

- ◆ Adonai...*Our God is miraculous, skillful.*

His steadfast love endures forever!

Read **Psalm 136:1-26**

How wonderful God is;

- ◆ Creation: vs. 5-9

- ◆ Deliverance: vs. 10-16

- ◆ Protection: vs. 17-25

- ◆ God of Heaven vs. 26

Read Psalm 136 and give thanks.

"JESUS IS THE SAME YESTERDAY, TODAY, AND FOREVER."

Hebrews 15:8

Finishing Grace

In scripture it says:

"God is the author and the finisher of my Faith." Anyone can **start** something; only a few can **finish** what they started:

- *A diet*

- *A marriage*

- *A lifetime dream*

- *A great purpose in life*

- *A commitment or goal in your life.*

Along the way we experience many **difficulties** and **hardships**:

These things only happen to discourage us.

They are put there to stop us from truly finishing what we started; by the evil one.

God says in Philippians:

"HE WHO BEGAN A GOOD WORK IN YOU WILL BE FAITHFUL TO COMPLETE IT."

God gives you the **Grace** to **Finish** your **Task!**

Set-backs only are there to keep us from finishing it.

- *Discouragement*
- *Self-pity*
- *I can't do it*
- *It will never come to be*
- *Injury*

Rely on God because when you feel like you're going under, God will take you over.

The closer we get to the finish, the steeper the mountain becomes.

"I CAN DO ALL THINGS THROUGH CHRIST WHO STRENGTHENS ME."

Philippians 4:13,

Fight the negative thoughts- it means you are getting closer to the finish line.

You're **one day** closer to the **FINISH** of what you started.

Adversity has to be expected but how you handle it will determine your **Destiny.**

God has made you to reach your **Destiny.**

God is truly the Author and the Finisher of our Faith.

Run The Race To The Finish

God's grace is sufficient for every one of us.

Never forget what God has enabled us to do. You must also remember when you are discouraged that,

"Greater is He that is in you; than he who is in the world." 1 John 4:4

Discuss this verse; who, why, what, how, and when...to you?

No Regrets

Regret will pull you down and affect you greatly!

Don't worry about regret:

Woulda, coulda or shoulda.

It will lead to :

➢ *Depression*

➢ *Guilt*

➢ *Shame*

Self-induced STRESS:

Depression, panic attacks, migraines, can't sleep, BUT most important, it draws you away from God.

If we run from God *REGRET* will overwhelm us.

There is nowhere that we can go, that God isn't there.

"GOD'S THOUGHTS ARE NOT OUR THOUGHTS."

ISAIAH 55:8,

Jesus loved us just as we were, that He died for us, and cares for us enough that He will not leave us that way.

God brings us out of the **PIT of despair**.

He **will deliver** us from our regret of the past.

All we must do is ASK God for help!

"ASK, SEEK, AND KNOCK" MATTHEW 7:7,

Then...let...it...GO!

Encourage discussion on Matt 7:7.

1 Peter 5:8

"Resist the Devil and he will FLEE from you."

➣ Stand **Firm** against him. Avoid his temptations.

➣ God **alone** has already defeated the devil, our adversary, on our behalf.

➣ **Resist** and face the enemy.

➣ Be **firm** in your faith-stable and solid in your faith in God.

"..in my absence from you, I am with you in Spirit."

Colossians 2:5

"Encourage one another at all times"

1 Thessalonians 5:11

Tell your teammate:"I've got your back!".

Create a *__Phalanx:__* the way the soldiers of Rome fought together as a block.

Keep the rank; I've got your back.

Christ uses His word always to help His people.

1 Peter 5:8, *"The devil, your adversary, prowls around like a roaring lion seeking whom he can devour."* **RESIST Him!!!** (If you stand clear of the devil and resist him the devil cannot hurt you.)

WALK WITH THE KING AND BE A BLESSING.

Always stay in touch with God.

Praise Him all day long!

4 Steps Getting Back To God: *when you have fallen away*

1. *"Love the Lord, your God, with all your heart and soul."* Praise him with everything you have. (Are you doing that?)

2. *Talk with your God every day.* Relationships are built on communications. (Do you talk to God daily?)

3. *Trust God in everything you do for He can supply all your needs.* He has already provided. (Do you trust Him?)

4. *Be filled with peace because God has heard your cries.* He knows your needs, and is at work providing care for those who love Him and called according to His purpose. (Do you pray on all occasions, with all kinds of requests?)

"TRUST IN THE LORD WITH ALL YOUR HEART; LEAN NOT ON YOUR OWN UNDERSTAND-ING, BUT IN ALL YOUR WAYS ACKNOWLEDGE HIM, AND HE WILL MAKE YOUR PATHS STRAIGHT." Proverbs 3:5-6

Pray

1 Chronicles 7:14 reads…

"IF MY PEOPLE WHO ARE CALLED BY MY NAME…WILL HUMBLE THEMSELVES AND PRAY, AND SEEK MY FACE, AND TURN FROM THEIR WICKED WAYS, THEN I WILL HEAR THEIR PRAYERS IN HEAVEN AND WILL HEAL THEIR LAND."

Above all: *ALWAYS keep PRAYING!!*

Pray *continuously* for all requests and make them *known to God!*

Your prayers will help you develop a good relationship with God. If you do it **EVERYDAY!!**

Disciples of God: **Talk to God today.**

The secret formula for SUCCESS in life~ is to simply PRAY everyday!

What Does Your God Require Of You?

Our LOVE. Our BEST.

God expects nothing less!

He loves you unconditionally.

He sent HIS ONLY SON to die on the cross for us.

He will NEVER leave you nor FORSAKE you.

Jesus is the same yesterday, today, and forever.

3 things in: **Micah 6:8**

➢ *To always act justly. (Do what is **RIGHT**)*

➢ *To reflect His love, mercy, and grace.*

➢ *Keep walking after Him & Almighty God will richly bless all of you.*

Praising God All Of The Time

The deepest level of WORSHIP is praising God despite your pain.

Your praise should always be in your heart!

✤ *I will trust in the Lord forever; His praise will always be in my mouth.*
✤ *Thank God during your trials.*
✤ *Trust Him when you're tempted to lose hope.*
✤ *Love Him even when He seems so distant and so far away*

o At our lowest ~**God is our Hope!**
o At our darkest ~**God is our Light!**
o At our weakest~**God is our Strength!**
o At our saddest~**God is our Comforter!**

If God is for us, who can be against us? Always TRUST and OBEY GOD!

"GOD HAS PROMISED NEVER TO LEAVE US. NEVER TO FORSAKE US."

Hebrews 13:5

12 Ordinary Men

The **DISCIPLES** -the greatest team ever assembled

Jesus- the greatest coach that ever lived

All chosen by Jesus personally to share His message!

12 ordinary men led by God who changed the world!

As a follower of Jesus, you are:

✦ *The least*

✦ *The last*

✦ *The lost*

Ordinary people from different walks of life that God allowed to have power to do extraordinary things for the Kingdom of God.

Then you will become:

- ✦ *The most*

- ✦ *The first*

- ✦ *The found*

By the Spirit of the living God He made them

"..FISHERS OF MEN, AND SAID, 'COME FOLLOW ME.'"

God gave us His mercy and grace by His dying on the cross for the forgiveness of our SINS.

Salvation is for each and every one of us!

His unconditional love endures forever.

We serve a risen Savior because on the third day of death, He rose from the grave and appeared to Mary and His disciples.

40 days later, He ascended into Heaven to be seated at the right hand of the Father.

"He will come again in glory; to judge the living and the dead and His kingdom will have no end".

He is coming back for us all!

Matthew 28:19 The Great Commission~

"GO THEREFORE....."

Acts Chapter 1: Here is where you will find the "Apostles Mission?.

7 Things That God Detests

PROVERBS 6:16-19

1. Haughty eyes (brazen looks).

2. A lying tongue.

3. Hands that shed innocent blood.

4. A heart that devises wicked plans.

5. Feet that make haste to run to evil.

6. A false witness who breathes out lies.

7. One who sows discord among the people.

> *These are just simple warnings for winning teams. Always live your life to please God.*
>
> *Stay upright and Holy in the eyes of God and always seek His will and His ways for your Life.*

"...the Lord said: "Be Holy because I am Holy." 1 Peter 1:16

Who Is This Jesus?

1. He never wrote a book. ~ yet, all 66 books of the Bible are about Him.
2. He wasn't a licensed physician. ~ but, He healed many people with a multitude of different miracles.
3. He never held an office. ~ but, became the complete Savior of the world.
4. He never traveled more than 60 miles from his hometown or the place He was born~yet His gospel has been spread throughout the World.
5. He created the World and everything in it~ yet, He was not a scientist or inventor.
6. He never went to college. ~~ yet, two thousand years after His death people still worship His principles.
7. All time; as we understand it; is predicated on His entire life.
8. Just a carpenter by trade.

9. Sacrificed by His Father to die on the Cross for all of us.

WHO is this Jesus?
Jesus is the one who is, the one who was, and the one who is to come again!

✣ *What would you say about Him?*

✣ *The world constantly wants to reject His will and His ways for their lives.*

✣ *We reject the Power and the Glory of Almighty God.*

God's Word says: *"For thine is the Power and the Glory forever and ever. Everything in Heaven and on Earth are Yours.").* 1 Chronicles 29:11

  "Scripture tells us our God is able." **2 Cor. 9:8**

  "Nothing is impossible with God!" **Matt.19:26**

  "If God is for us than who could be against us?"

Romans 8:31

Only He can make the weak be Strong
Only He can make the Poor become Rich.

Only He can set the worst sinner Free.

DO NOT be ashamed of the Gospel. ~ He is the King of Kings and the Lord of Lords.

It all goes back to the cross and what the Almighty God did for all of us there.

- *Can you honestly say that you know Christ as your Personal Savior?*
- *All you need to do is to Pray, the Sinners Prayer below:*

Pray with me now:

Dear Lord;

I believe that you are the Son of God and that you died on the cross for the forgiveness of all my sins. On the third day you rose from the grave in accordance with the scriptures). I ask you to come into my heart; and I want you to be my Lord and Savior of my life. Forgive me of all my sin and make me a "New Creature" in you. Come into my Heart today.

AMEN

That's who Jesus really is~

He died on the Cross for the complete forgiveness
of everyone's SIN.

Christ is the Savior of the World!

JESUS Is The Same
Yesterday, Today And Forever

Jesus promised that He will never leave us nor forsake us. (*These are just two of His 3,600 promises in His word.*)

Almighty God has always delivered on every PROMISE that He made!

-That is our *Blessed Assurance* that we can depend on.

John 16:33, tells us that *" we have endless trials and troubles but our Savior has overcome the world."*

In all circumstances of life we should be quick to praise the Lord in all that we do.

Not only do we need to read God's word; but, do what it says.

Meditate on it.

Carry Your Own Cross

Carry your own Cross and follow Him giving Him the glory and honor.

If things are going Great; Praise His name. If things are getting Tough; do the same.

In real times of difficulty, we forget that. We need to make time to give God the Glory. God deserves all the praise we can give Him, all the time.

Lest we forget; God is in control!

God controls yesterday, today, and tomorrow.

Praise God

....IN ALL CIRCUMSTANCES

"I will bless the Lord at all times. His Praise will always be on my lips." **Psalm 34:1**

Praise God in everything you do. Whether you have plenty or whether you have none; always give God the glory and honor due His Holy Name.

The God on the mountain is still God in the valley.

Whether in calm or crises, give the Lord the Praise He is due.

Good News & Bad News

Romans 6:23:

"For the wages of Sin is Death; but, the Gift of God is Eternal Life in Christ Jesus our Lord."

It contains 20 very important words: we need to know.

- Memorize it.

- It is one of the most informative and inspirational verses in the Bible, but, it contains **Good News and Bad News.**

Let's talk about: **The Bad News First**

- The wages of Sin is Death. (Period)

- What part of that don't you understand?

- A wage is something you get for doing something. (Salary or hourly rate)

- The Bad News in Sins case: is **DEATH**.

  - Total separation from God.

  - A huge price to pay for your Sins; but Payday is coming soon.

Romans 3:23 *".. all have sinned and fallen short of the glory of God. ".*

However, God will forgive us all for that and guarantees eternal life.

Another name for the Gospel is **"Good News"**. Know what it is!

The **Good News** is **Eternal Life.** That means life with Christ forever.

- God's great free gift to us is **Forever** and ever.

- To spend **Eternity** with our creator.

- To live forever with our **Savior, the Lord Jesus Christ.**

- It's not a thought or a myth; it's a **Promise from Almighty God.**

- That **Good News** is as good at it gets.

- Know what God has promised; *all of us who Believe in Eternal Life!*

  Remember this:

- We need preachers who preach that **Hell** is still hot and separates us from God.

- That **Heaven** is real; God has prepared a place for us.

- That **Sin** is still wrong, we must obey the Lord's will for our lives.

- That the **Bible is God's word-** Know it, Live it, Believe it, Trust it.

And that Jesus Christ is the only way to Salvation.

- All has been completed at the **CROSS**; Jesus died and rose on the third day for each one us

- **Eternal Life** awaits us; as our reward.

Let's get serious right now.

Have you accepted Jesus Christ as your Lord and Savior?

Are you saved? Can you say with conviction that "Jesus is Lord" in all my Life?
I will not perish but have Everlasting Life.

Which way are you running? Toward Him or Away from Him?

- **Is the Lord tugging at your heart today?**

- **What are you waiting for?**

- It's something **WE ALL MUST DO!**
- There is always room at the CROSS for you today

Please make your decision today! Let's do it NOW!

Pray this prayer:

Lord Jesus, I want you to be Lord and Savior of my Life. Please forgive me of all my sin. Teach me your will and your ways to live my life for you. Live within my heart.

In Jesus name….

If you prayed that Prayer, and believe it,

~~~~~You are Saved~~~~~~

Thanks be to God!

The Mustard Seed

Mark 4:30-32; Matthew 12:31; Luke 13:18

Jesus talked to His disciples in Parables to provide them with a lesson to always remember.

Jesus gave them the parable of the Mustard Seed in **Mark 4:30**

FAITH:

"Again He said, "What shall we say the Kingdom of God is like, or what parable shall we use to describe it? It is like a mustard seed, which is the smallest of all seeds on earth. Yet, when planted, it grows and becomes the largest of all garden plants, with such big branches that the birds can perch in its shade."

Isn't it strange that the smallest of all the garden seeds will grow to the size of a tree with branches?

Thus it is with our **Faith**; and Jesus used this parable to make that analogy with His disciples.

What an example to illustrate how our faith can grow and prosper!

Use it; as an example of your own **FAITH.**

Let it grow big and large!

God Hears Your Prayer

He knows, He sees, He cares!

"For I know the plans I have for you. Plans to prosper you and give you hope. Plans to give you a future."

Jeremiah 29:11

Challenge yourself to talk to God everyday!

1. When God answers your prayers- *He is increasing your faith.*

2. When God delays your prayers- *He is increasing your patience in Him.*

3. If God doesn't answer your prayer- *He has something better for you, so Trust in Him.*

4. Thank God for your unanswered prayers-

He has a better plan for your Life.

God will take your mess and He will turn it into your Message!

Encourage your teammates in prayer, as you do during the game.

"This then is how you should pray"

Matthew 6:9

Psalm 55:22

"Cast all your cares on the Lord and He will sustain you; He will never let the Righteous be shaken."

This Psalm is biblical proof that "**good guys**" do finish first.

When you live upright and holy, it proves to God that you are indeed, **RIGHTEOUS**. *God promised not to let you fall or be shaken.*

God is always there when we need Him.

David said *"…when I call on you; you hear my prayers and answer them.".*
Always Trust in the Lord Your God.

God is always listening~~~talk to Him every day.
He cares for you with unconditional LOVE.

Be like David: *"Be a man after God's own Heart.".*

Examine Yourself

Psalm 19:14; *"May the words of my mouth and the meditations in my heart be forever acceptable in your sight; oh Lord my Rock and my Redeemer."*

John was chosen by God for great purpose of the Kingdom. John was the only disciple not martyred.

He wrote 5 books of the **New Testament:**

~ **St. John; 1ˢᵗ John; 2ⁿᵈ John; 3ʳᵈ John, and the book of REVELATION.**

Book of John's Gospel of Christ;

- Gives introductions to us.

- John was God's Beloved disciple.

- Easiest book of the Bible to read; a great place to start reading in the Bible.

- James and John "the sons of thunder".

- Bold and brash disciples of Christ.

- **Tells who Jesus really is; and His purpose here on earth**

- **Tells of the 7 miracles that Jesus performed in this book alone:**

Wedding at Cana. The 1st miracle of Jesus.

Healing of the Official's Son, "Your son will live."

Healing at the pool of Bethesda.

The feeding of the 5,000 from 5 loaves and 2 fish.

Healing of the man born blind, on the Sabbath. *(This upset all the clerics.)*

Jesus walks on water to the disciples on the Sea of Galilee during a storm.

The raising of Lazarus from the dead. That was specifically planned to Glorify the Power of God.

Mary and Martha testify to that fact that Lazarus had been dead for 3 or 4 days.

- **Tells of the divinity of Christ Jesus. Teaches us Christ's purpose on earth. Sent from God the Father to die on the cross for our Sins.**

Most quoted verse of the Bible:

John 3:16; *"For God so loved the world that He sent His only begotten son that whosoever would believe in Him shall not perish; but have everlasting life."*

John 1:1; *"The Word of God; and the Word was with God...."*

John 1:14; *"the word became flesh and dwelt among us"*, (the greatest gift ever given).

The Message of the Cross is abundantly clear. It's all about the message of the Cross!

GOD SENT HIS SON TO DIE FOR OUR SINS!

The Gospel In 26 Words

John 3:16; *"For God so loved the world that He gave his only begotten son that whosoever would believe in him would not perish; but have everlasting life."*

- The most quoted verse in the Bible

- The entire GOSPEL in 26 words

- Are you able to do that? It's done for you!

- The entire Gospel in one verse

- The Message of the Cross explained to you

Is it common or uncommon?

John 3:16 broken down:

God's cause *"For God so loved the world..."*

- God's love for you is the motivating cause of Salvation.

- He first loved us and gave His life for us; for the total forgiveness of our Sins.

- Salvation's COST: *"..that He gave his only begotten son..."*

- Salvation for you; with the free pardoning of your SINS.

- *Freedom is never free; but is always bought with blood.*

- Salvation is not possible without the blood of Christ; sacrificed at the CROSS.

- **Romans 5:8;** God demonstrates his own love for us; in that, while we were still sinners; Christ died on the cross for us.

Salvation has CONDITIONS:

- *"that whosoever believes in Him..."* That includes every single person reading this.

- No adjectives apply: young old, black, white, big, small, male and female, etc.

- **Acts 16:30;** A Phillippian jailer asked Paul~~ *"What must I do to be saved?"*.

- Paul answered: ***"Believe on the Lord Jesus Christ, and you will be saved."***

- Anyone who justly calls on the Name of the Lord will be saved."

- We pay no price or cost for our Salvation: Jesus paid it all; on the Cross.

- Salvations **CONSEQUENCES:** *"…should not perish but have everlasting life…"*

- Those without Christ are perishing; but those in Christ will have everlasting life.

Remember that,

"the wages of Sin is Death.."

God's love reaches out to us; no matter where we are or who we are!!!

Let's break it down further;

- For God *the greatest Lover of Humanity.*

- so loved *the greatest degree.*

- the world *the greatest company.*

- That He gave *the greatest act.*

- His only begotten son *the greatest gift.*

- That whosoever *the greatest opportunity*

- Believes *the greatest simplicity.*

- In Him *the greatest attraction.*

- will not perish *the greatest promise.*

- But *the greatest difference.*
- Have *the greatest certainty.*
- Everlasting life *the greatest possession.*

God knows you; God loves you; God has a wonderful plan for your life. (*Not everyone believes that.*)

"IT IS WRITTEN"

"FOR I KNOW THE PLANS I HAVE FOR YOU. PLANS TO PROSPER YOU AND GIVE YOU HOPE. PLANS TO GIVE YOU A FUTURE. **Jeremiah 29:11**

Good Guys Finish 1st

"Blessed is the man who does not walk in the counsel of the wicked or stand in the way of sinners or sit in the seat of mockers. But his delight is in the law of the Lord and on his law he meditates day and night.

He is like a tree planted by the streams of water, which yields it fruit in season and whose leaf does not wither. Whatever he does prospers.

Not so with the Wicked! They are like chaff that the wind blows away.

Therefore, the wicked will not stand in the judgement, nor sinners in the assembly of the righteous.

For the Lord watches over the way of the righteous, but the way of the wicked will perish.".

PSALM 1

Proverbs 3:5-6

"TRUST IN THE LORD WITH ALL YOUR HEART;

LEAN NOT ON YOUR OWN UNDERSTANDING;

BUT IN ALL YOUR WAYS ACKNOWLEDGE HIM AND

HE WILL MAKE YOUR PATHS STRAIGHT."

TRUST IN THE LORD.

The Psalms & James

Psalm 46:10 *"Be still and know that I am God…"*

Psalm 113:3*"From the rising of the Sun to the going down of the same; the Lord's name is to be praised…"*

Psalm 146:5 *"Blessed is he whose hope in in the Lord his God…"*

Psalm 8:9 *"O, Lord how majestic is your name in all the earth…"*

Psalm 123:1 *"I lift my eyes to you, to you whose throne is in heaven…"*

Psalm 1:6 *"For the Lord watches over the way of the righteous…"*

Psalm 112:4 *"Even in darkness; light dawns for the upright…"*

Psalm 34:5 *"Those, who look to Him are radiant; their faces are never covered with shame…"*

Psalm 18:28 *"You O Lord, keep my lamp burning, my God turns my darkness into light…"*

Psalm 97:6 *"The heavens proclaim His righteousness; and all the peoples see His glory."*

Psalm 96:7 *"Splendor and majesty are before Him; strength and glory are in His sanctuary…"*

Psalm 56:4 *"In God I trust; I will not be afraid…"*

Psalm 55:22 *"Cast all your cares on the Lord and He will sustain you; He will never let the righteous fall…"*

James 1:26 *"If any man claims to be religious and does not watch his tongue…."*

James 3:9-10 *"With the tongue we 'Praise our Lord' and Father, and with it we curse men…"*

James 3:1 *"We who teach will be judged more strictly…"*

End Times

"Blessed is the one who reads aloud the words of this prophecy, and blessed are those who hear it and take to heart what is written in it, because the time is near."

Revelation 1:3

Where are you going when you die?

I don't want to look for an undertaker. I want an overtaker to get me to heaven!

I don't want to see the antichrist. I want to see Jesus Christ and spend eternity with Him.

I won't look for a hole in the ground but a hole in the sky.

Make ready the time is near!

Do you know where you are headed when you die?

Make sure you know it with certainty!

THE END =
THE BOOK
OF
REVELATION

James 1:2-4

It's about **FAITH!**

"Consider it pure joy, my brother, whenever you face trials of many kinds, because you know that the testing of your FAITH develops perseverance.

Perseverance must finish its work so that you might become mature and complete, not lacking in anything."

Hebrews 11:1 *"Now faith is being sure of what we hoped for; and certain of what we do not see."*

BELIEVE:

Hebrews 10:23 *"Let us hold unwaveringly to the HOPE we profess, for He who PROMISED is FAITHFUL."*

Psalm 119:11

CHANGE YOUR LIFE WITH 15 POWERFUL WORDS.

"I have hidden your word in my heart that I might not sin against you."

- Memorize God's Word
- Hide it in your heart
- Know it, that you might not sin against God.

The Most Important:

Psalm 19:14 *"May the words of my mouth and the meditation of my heart, be acceptable in your sight, O Lord, my strength, and my redeemer."*.

- God doesn't want a Share of your life;
  He wants a controlling interest!
- God didn't give Moses the 10 Suggestions-
  He gave the 10 Commandments!

• LIVE IT

• Follow the word

• Don't just hear it! Do it.

Trust In The Lord: Believe In His Promises

•**To fail to believe** in God, is the epitome of insult.

• **To doubt Him** is to suggest that He is possibly a liar.

•It is to put a plot on His character, to **blemish the integrity of his Holy Name.**

•**It is to suggest that God will not do** what He said that He would do.

•**To worry about what God promised** to fix is an insult against God.

•**To think that you can deal with something that God told you not to worry about** is to suggest that you have more power and intellect than God.

•**It is idolatry** and you should ask for God's forgiveness. **God told us not to worry. He will give provisions.**

Psalm 43:5; Matthew 6:25-26

He provides for the sparrows in the sky, so He
will provide for you and I.

Matthew 6:26

"Trust in the Lord with all your heart...."

Psalm 55:22

*"Cast all your cares on the Lord and He will strengthens
you. He will never let the righteous fall...."*

Proverbs 3:5

*"Trust in the Lord with all your heart and
lean not on your own understanding; in
all your ways submit to him,
and He will make your paths straight."*

25 Bible Verses About Prayer

1 Thes 5:16-18   Joy and gratitude

"*Rejoice always, pray continually, give thanks in all circumstances; for this is God's will for you in Christ Jesus.*"

Philippians 4:6-7   Gratitude, worry & fear

"*Do not be anxious about anything, but in every situation, by prayer and petition, with thanksgiving, present your requests to God. And the peace of God, which transcends all understanding, will guard your hearts and your minds in Christ Jesus.*"

1 John 5:14   Trust & Listening

"*This is the confidence we have in approaching God; that if we ask anything according to His will, He hears us.*"

Colossians 4:2   Gratitude

"Devote yourselves to prayer, being watchful and thankful."

Mark 11:24   Faith & receiving

"Therefore I tell you, whatever you ask for in prayer, believe that you have received it, and it will be yours."

Jeremiah 29:12   Worship & Listening

"Then you will call on me and come and pray to me, and I will listen to you."

Romans 12:12   Joy & patience

"Be joyful, patient in affliction, faithful in prayer."

Matthew 6:7   Speaking

"And when you pray, do not keep on babbling like pagans, for they think they will be heard because of their many words."

Psalm 145:18   Trust & Reliability

"The Lord is near to all who call on Him, to all who call on Him in truth.

Jeremiah 33:3   Understanding & Listening

"Call to me and I will answer you and tell you great and unsearchable things you do not know."

Matthew 18:20   Jesus & Community

"For where two or three gather in my name, there am I with them."

Hebrews 4:16   Mercy

"Let us then approach God's throne of grace with confidence, so that we may receive mercy and find grace to help us in our time of need."

Matthew 6:6   Reward & Father

"But when you pray, go into your room, close the door and pray to your Father, who is unseen. Then your Father, who sees what is done in secret, will reward you."

Psalm 18:6   Speaking & Listening

"In my distress I called to the Lord; I cried to my God for help. From His temple, He heard my voice; my cry came before Him, into His ears."

James 1:6   Trust & Faith

"But when you ask, you must believe and not doubt, because the one who doubts is like a wave of the sea, blown and tossed by the wind."

James 5:16   Righteousness & Healing

"Therefore, confess your sins to each other and pray for each other so that you may be healed. The prayer of a righteous person is powerful and effective."

1 John 5:15   Trust & Listening

"And if we know that he hears us – whatever we ask—we know that we have what we asked of Him."

Luke 6:27-28   Obedience & Blessing

"But to you who are listening I say; Love your enemies, do good to those who hate you, bless those who curse you, pray for those who mistreat you."

Acts 16:25   Worship & Listening

"About midnight Paul and Silas were praying and singing hymns to God and the other prisoners were listening to them."

John 15:16   Obedience & Calling

"You did not choose me, but I chose you and appointed you so that you might go and bear fruit—fruit that will last—and so that whatever you ask in my name the Father will give you."

Acts 1:14   Community

"They all joined together constantly in prayer, along with the women and Mary the mother of Jesus, and with His brothers."

James 4:2   Sin & Desires

"You desire but do not have, so you kill. You covet but you cannot get what you want, so you quarrel and fight. You do not have because you do not ask God."

1 Peter 4:7   Second Coming & Rest

"The end of all things is near. Therefore, be alert and of sober mind so that you may pray."

John 14:13   Jesus & the Father

"And I will do whatever you ask in my name, so that the Father may be glorified in the Son."

"I cried out to Him with my mouth; His praise was on my tongue."

Read more bible verses about:

Listening

Worship

Trust

Speaking

A PRAYER FOR YOU

"I said a prayer for you today
And know God must have heard.

I felt the answer in my heart
Although He spoke no word.

I didn't ask for wealth or fame
I know you wouldn't mind

I asked Him to send treasures
Of a far more lasting kind.
I asked that He'd be near you
At the start of each new day To
grant you health and blessings
And friends to share your way.

I asked for happiness for you
In all things great and small.

But it was for His loving care
I prayed the most of all."

-Author Unknown

20 Verses To Memorize

John 3:16 (KNJV): *"For God so loved the world that He gave His only begotten Son, that whoever believes in Him should not perish but have everlasting life."*

1 John 1:19 (NIV): *"If we confess our sins, He is faithful and just and will forgive us our sins and purify us from all unrighteousness."*

Romans 6:23 (KJV): *"For the wages of sin is death; but the gift of God is eternal life through Jesus Christ our Lord."*

Ephesians 2:8-9 (NIV): *"For it is by grace you have been saved, through faith –and this not from yourselves, it is the gift of God… not by works, so that no one can boast."*

Galatians 2:20 (NIV): *"I have been crucified with Christ and I no longer live, but Christ lives in me. The life I live in the body, I live by faith in the Son of God, who loved me and gave Himself for me."*

2 Corinthians 5:17 (NLT): *"Anyone who belongs to Christ has become a new person. The old life is gone; a new life has begun!"*

Philippians 1:6 (NIV): *"Being confident of this, that He who began a good work in you will carry it on to completion until the day of Christ Jesus."*

Philippians 4:13 (NKJV): *I can do all things through Christ who strengthens me."*

Matthew 28:19-20 (NIV): *"Therefore go and make disciples of all nations, baptizing them in the name of the Father and the Son and of the Holy Spirit…and teaching them to obey everything I have commanded you. And surely, I am with you always, to the very end of the age."*

Luke 10:27 (NIV): *"Love the Lord your God with all your heart, with all your soul, and with all your strength and with all your mind ..and, Love your neighbor as yourself."*

John 14:6 (NIV): *"I am the way and the truth and the life. No one comes to the Father except through me."*

John 15:5 (NIV): *"I am the vine; you are the branches. If a man remains in me and I in him, he will bear much fruit; apart from me you can do nothing."*

Matthew 11:28 (NIV): *"Come to me, all you who are weary and burdened, and I will give you rest."*

Isaiah 26:3 (NKJV): *You will keep him in perfect peace, whose mind is stayed on You, because he trusts in You."*

1 Peter 5:7 (NIV): *"Cast all your anxiety on Him because He cares for you."*

Philippians 4:6-7 (NIV): *"Do not be anxious about anything, but in everything, by prayer and petition, with thanksgiving, present your requests to God...And the peace of God, which transcends all understanding, will guard your hearts and your minds in Christ Jesus."*

Isaiah 41:10 (NKJV): *"Fear not, for I am with you; be not dismayed, for I am your God. I will strengthen you, yes, I will help you, I will uphold you with My righteous right hand."*

Matthew 6:33 (NJKV): *"But seek first the kingdom of God and His righteousness, and all these things shall be added to you."*

Proverbs 3:5-6 (NKJV): *"Trust in the LORD with all your heart, and lean not on your own understanding;, in all your ways acknowledge Him, and He shall direct your paths."*

Psalm 119:105 (NIV): *Your word is a lamp to my feet and a light for my path."*

43 Scriptures About Faith

Hebrews 13:5: *"Let your character be free from the love of money, being content with what you have; for He Himself has said "NEVER WILL I LEAVE YOU; NEVER WILL I FORSAKE YOU."*

Deuteronomy 4:9: *"Only give heed to yourself and keep your soul diligently, lest you forget the things which your eyes have seen, and lest they depart from your heart all the days of your life; but make them known to your sons and your grandsons."*

Psalm 118:24: *"This is the day which the LORD has made, let us rejoice and be glad in it."*

Psalm 18:2: *"The Lord, is my rock, my fortress and my deliverer; my God is my Rock, in whom I take refuge, my shield and the horn of my salvation, my stronghold."*

1 Thessalonians 5:36: *"Rejoice always, pray without ceasing, in everything give thanks; for this is God's will for you in Christ Jesus."*

Exodus 3:14: *"And God said to Moses, 'I AM WHO I AM;' and He said this 'you shall say to the sons of Israel, I AM has sent me to you.'"*

Psalm 100:4-5: *"Enter His gates with thanksgiving, (and) His courts with praise. Give thanks to Him; Bless His Name. For the LORD is good, His loving kindness is everlasting, and His faithfulness to all generations."*

Matthew 18:19: *"Again, I say to you, that if two of you agree on earth about anything, that they may ask, it shall be done for them by my Father who is in Heaven."*

Psalm 56:8-9: *"Ascribe to the Lord the glory of His name, bring an offering, and come into his courts. Worship the LORD in holy attire; tremble before Him, all the earth."*

Psalm 52:9: *"I will give Thee thanks forever, for what You have done I will always praise you in the presence of Your faithful people. And I will hope in Your name, for Your name is good."*

Luke 6:47-48: *"Everyone who comes to me, and hears my words, and acts upon them I will show you whom he* is like. He is like a man building a house who dug deep and laid a foundation upon the rock and when the flood rose, the torrent burst against that house and could not shake it, because it had been well built."

Ezekiel **34:26**: *"And I will make them and places around my hill a blessing and I will cause showers to come down in their season. They will be showers of blessing."*

Hebrews 4:16: *"Let us therefore draw near with confidence to the throne of grace. That we may receive mercy and may find grace to help in time of need."*

Hebrews 11:3: *"By faith we understand that the worlds were prepared by the word of God, so that what is seen was not made out of things which are visible."*

1 Chronicles 29: 12-13: *"Both riches and honor (come) from Thee, and Thou dost rule over all, and in thy hand is power and might and it lies in Thy hand to make great and to strengthen everyone. Now therefore, our God we thank Thee, and praise Thy glorious name."*

James 1:12: *"Blessed is a man who perseveres under trial, for once he has been approved, he will receive the* *crown of life, which (The LORD) has promised to those who love him."*

Romans 14:19: *"So then let us pursue the things which make for peace and the building up of one another."*

Proverbs 3:7-8: *"Do not be wise in your own eyes. Fear the Lord and turn away from evil. It will be healing to your body, and refreshment to your bones."*

Proverbs 10:12: *"Hatred stirs up strife; But love covers all transgressions."*

Colossians 3:9-10: *"Do not lie to one another since you laid aside the old self with its (evil) practices and have put on the new self who is being renewed to a true knowledge according to the image of the one who created him."*

Revelation 4:11: *"Worthy art thou, our Lord and our God, to receive glory and honor and power; for thou didst create all things and because of thy will they existed and were created."*

Isaiah 43:2: *"When you pass through the waters I will be with you. And through the rivers, they will not over-*

flow you. When you walk through the fire, you will not be scorched, nor will the flame burn you."

Proverbs 18:22: *"He who finds a wife finds a good thing and obtains favor from the Lord."*

Deuteronomy 10:14: *"Behold, to the Lord your God belong heaven and the highest heavens, the earth and all that is in it."*

Psalm 89:11: *"The heavens are Thine, the earth also is Thine; the world and all it contains, thou has founded them."*

Psalm 22:16: *"For dogs have surrounded me, a band of evildoers has encompassed me; they pierced my hands and my feet."*

Exodus 15:11: *"Who is like Thee among the gods, O Lord? Who is like Thee, majestic in holiness, Awesome in praises, working wonders?"*

Romans 12:2: *"And do not be conformed to this world, but be transformed by the renewing of your mind, that you may prove what the will of God is, that which is good and acceptable and perfect."*

Ephesians 5:1: *"Therefore be imitators of God, as beloved children."*

Romans 12:14: *"Bless those who persecute you; bless and curse not."*

Luke 17:3: *"Be on your guard if your brother sins, rebuke him, and if he repents, forgive him."*

1 Corinthians 3:16: *"Do you not know that you are a temple of God, and (that) the Spirit of God dwells in you?"*

Psalm 28:7: *"The Lord is my strength and my shield; My heart trusts in Him, and I am helped; Therefore, my heart exults, and with my song I shall thank Him."*

James 4:8: *"Draw near to God and He will draw near to you. Cleanse your hands, you sinners, and purify your hearts, you double-minded."*

Romans 8:32: *"He who did not spare His own son, but delivered him up for us all, how will He not also with Him freely give us all things?"*

John 1:14: *"And the Word became flesh, and dwelt among us, and we beheld His glory. Glory as of the only begotten from the Father, full of grace and truth."*

Psalm 54:1: *"Save me, O God, by thy name, and vindicate me by thy power."*

1 Timothy 6:12: *"Fight the good fight of faith, take hold of the eternal life to which you were called, and you made the good confession in the presence of many witnesses."*

1 Corinthians 13:4-5: *"Love is patient, love is kind (and) it is not jealous; love does not brag (and) is not arrogant. does not act unbecoming; it does not seek its own, is not provoked, does not take into account a wrong suffered."*

Psalm 20:5: *"We will sing for joy over your victory, and in the name of our God we will set up our banners. "May the Lord fulfill all your petitions."*

Philippians 4:13: *"I can do all things through Him who strengthens me."*

Hebrews 2:1: *"For this reason, we must pay much closer attention to what we have heard, least we drift away (from it)."*

1 John 4:8: *"The one who does not love does not know God, for God is Love."*

Erie Invocation

Friends, this is an actual prayer I prayed for an arena football team in Erie, PA:

"Would you please bow your heads?

Almighty God, we thank you.

Thank you Lord, that we live in the United States of America. The greatest country in the world!

Bless each team that stands before us. May they play their best today; Lord please keep them free from serious injury, as they perform their talents, today.

Please bless each person and family here that will witness this athletic contest, bless them with your **Loving Hand of Grace and Mercy**—in your **Holy and Gracious Name** we pray."

Amen.

The Glory & Grace Of God

God's Grace is God's best; for man's worst.

HE CAME DOWN TO US TO FORGIVE ALL OUR SIN.   (The message of the Cross)

"All have sinned and fallen short of the Glory of God." **Romans 3:23**

Nobody is perfect- like Jesus!

The evil one loves to throw this up into our face and cause fear and doubt in our everyday life.

Just doubt can make us stray **OFF TRACK**. Pull us away from serving God and sideline us from true Worship to the King of Kings.

The evil one is cunning; he is the father of lies and so easily we fall into his snare.

The devil will pull us away from serving our God and King.

SIN leads us to shame; shame leads us to guilt; and guilt leads us into condemnation.

The scripture tells us:

"There is now no condemnation for those who are in Christ Jesus."

If we believe His word; we stay free from the devil's snare and cannot be trapped.

"Resist the devil and he will flee from you."

"Jesus is the same yesterday, today, and forever."

God has promised Never to leave us; nor forsake us.

Hold on to God's sacred promises.

- There are more than 3,600 promises in God's Holy word and He has **NEVER** failed to deliver on any of them!

- Trust and obey; for there is no other way!

- An old spiritual says something to the fact:

"It is no secret; what God can do. What He has done for others; He will do for you. With arms wide open; He will pardon you." *

IT IS NO SECRET, WHAT OUR GOD CAN DO!

*Excerpt From A song by Russ Hamblin

The Valley Of The Dry Bones

If you can believe it in Faith—God can perform it.

The Valley of the Dry Bones :**Ezekiel 37**

This chapter represents the people of God of Israel who disobeyed God in all they did. They died for it. They were destroyed in battle. There was nothing left of them but dry bones laying in a Valley.

God told the prophet Ezekiel to prophesy to these bones and speak life into them.

They were just dry bones.

As he prayed, the bones began to develop suet on them and tissue began to form. The bones began to form life in them. The bones began to have life. They became an Army again.

Resurrected in life by Almighty God!

Now they came to life and had purpose.

All of this was done by God through the prophet Ezekiel in the Valley of dry bones.

WHAT A MIRACLE OF GOD!

He is able.

The Lord gave life to the dry bones for the purpose to **glorify** the **Kingdom of God.**

The Lord said to Ezekiel,

"SON OF MAN, NOW THESE PEOPLE WILL KNOW THE POWER OF ALMIGHTY GOD."

If the Lord can resurrect dry bones to fight, will He not help you?

You just have to ask!!

The Chain Breaker

Christian music artist, Zach Williams wrote a song called **"Chain Breaker"**:

"If you got Pain;
He is the Pain Taker
If you feel lost;
He is the way maker
If you need Freedom; Saving
He is a Prison-Shaking Savior
If you got Chains;
He is a chain breaker"

Jesus has paid the price at the Cross for your sins.

He broke the chains of Sin in your life.

There is power in the name of Jesus.

.

"If you feel lost;
He is a way-maker."

JESUS IS THE WAY, THE TRUTH AND THE LIFE.

Trust in the Lord with all your heart.

He will deliver you from it all and breakyour chains.

The F.R.O.G. Concept

An acronym for;

"Fully Rely On God"

In any challenge in life (athletic contests included) you must always remember to:

Fully. Rely. On. God.

God must really have a great sense of humor to use the FROG concept to keep us focused on what's really important.

The simplicity of the ugly little frog serves to remind us of the awesome power of God.

What a great reminder of a very important concept.

SIMPLICITY

Always focus on;

Fully. Rely. On. God.

The FROG concept.

You will never go wrong with that choice.

Fully. Rely. On. God.

'Trust in the Lord with all your heart; lean not on your own understanding but in all your ways acknowledge Him and He will make your paths straight.'

- Proverbs 3: 5-6

Praise God from whom all blessings flow.

F.R.O.G.

Jake Olsen

Jake Olsen #61 for USC snapped the extra point for USC late in the game against the Western Michigan Broncos in the 2017 football season.

Jake Olsen is BLIND. He lost vision in both eyes due to cancer. The loss of his sight did not hold him back from playing high school football and to make it as a walk-on with University of Southern California.

Jake was the first blind person to be led on the field by a teammate to snap the football for the extra point try.

Jake's snap was good and so was the extra point.

USC won the football game 49-31 by pulling away in a 4th quarter lead .

What a story of courage and perseverance for young Jake Olsen to successfully complete this task in a NCAA football game!

He is an inspiration to others who are struggling with their very own circumstances of disappointment or despair.

What a story!
WHAT A GOD WE SERVE!!

"I can do all things through Christ who strengthens me. "

Philippians 4:13

Great Moments with God

We all have special moments with God.

Here are some great ones:

1. Praise God
   In the difficult moments.

2. Seek God
   In the quiet moments.

3. Worship God
   In the painful moments.

4. Trust God
   In every moment.

5. Thank God
   for giving us these moments.

God is always there for us 24/7 !

There is no place that we can go that He isn't beside us!

He has already promised that He will NEVER leave us nor forsake us!

He always hears the cries of His people!

If we don't quit on **GOD** He won't quit on us!

GOD
IS
GREAT !

About the Author

Jim Gillespie was born in Ashtabula, Ohio. He graduated high school 1965, after setting school records for the shot put and discus (the shot put record has yet to be broken as of the printing of this book!) .

Jim then went on to Ohio University from 1965 to 1969, where he played football and wrestled. He graduated in 1969, with a BSED in Education. Heading back to his high school alma mater, Jim accepted a teaching and coaching position in three varsity sports. After 6 years, Jim and his wife, Mary Frances and their 3 children moved an hour away to another high school where he coached football, wrestling, track, and girl's fast pitch softball.

In 1986, Jim left teaching entirely and joined the New York Life Insurance Company as an agent and then became Sales Office manager . He was eventually transferred to create the Davenport, Iowa Office. Years later, Jim became a Safety Director for Defiance Metal Products Company in Defiance, Ohio and 5 of their plants. He eventually retired.

Jim and Mary Frances then relocated to Meadville, Pennsylvania, to be with their 3 children and their families. Especially, their grandchildren, **Luca, Joey and Carlee**- to whom this book is dedicated.

Though retired, Jim continues to be a chaplain for college and professional sports teams. He has worked for AAA baseball, CBA basketball, College Football and the PIFL Arena Football teams.

In 2016, Jim Gillespie was inducted into the Ashtabula Touchdown Club Hall of Fame- one of Northeast Ohio's greatest honors for an athlete.

In his induction ceremony speech, Jim said,

"God has truly blessed me with the privilege of being involved in football. Football has been my life."

"I am truly yours in Christ",

Jim Gillespie

Made in the USA
Columbia, SC
14 April 2019